Wiccan Magick
for Beginners

Wiccan Magick for Beginners

A Guide to Spells, Rites, and Customs

Lady Sabrina

CITADEL PRESS
Kensington Publishing Corp.
www.kensingtonbooks.com

To all the members of Our Lady of Enchantment,
both past and present.

To Autumn and Aristaeus, without whom it would
not be possible to write a book.

Thank you.

CITADEL PRESS books are published by

Kensington Publishing Corp.
850 Third Avenue
New York, NY 10022

All Kensington titles, imprints, and distributed lines are available at special
quantity discounts for bulk purchases for sales promotions, premiums, fund
raising, educational, or institutional use. Special book excerpts or customized
printings can also be created to fit specific needs. For details, write or phone
the office of the Kensington special sales manager: Kensington Publishing Corp.,
850 Third Avenue, New York, NY 10022, attn: Special Sales Department,
phone 1-800-221-2647.

Citadel Press and the Citadel logo are trademarks of Kensington Publishing Corp.

First printing July 2001

10 9 8 7 6 5 4 3 2 1

Printed in the United States of America

Cataloging data for this title may be obtained from the Library of Congress.

ISBN 0-8065-2153-8

Contents

Preface

Ten years ago, when I wrote my first book *Reclaiming the Power* (Llewellyn Publications, 1992), there were very few *good* books available on Wicca or Wiccan Magick. Since that time, Wicca has blossomed into one of the fastest growing spiritual systems in the country. There are dozens of books available on the subject of Wicca as a religion, but still very few that address the subject of magick itself.

Having taught Wicca for over twenty years, I can say with some authority, that most of the people who come to Wicca from other spiritual systems do so for the magick. Almost all religions in some way worship deity, celebrate high holy days, acknowledge life's major transitions, and provide social activities for their members. The one thing that most religions do not acknowledge is magick and the right of individuals to pursue happiness on their own.

In general, most mainstream religions teach that the individual must depend upon the grace of God (and the church) for the fulfillment of their desires. When an individual discovers that there is a religion, like Wicca, that encourages self-reliance through magick, they usually tend to get involved very quickly. They will invariably buy every book available on the subject, only to discover that magick has been relegated to an appendix. If time and space have been given to the subject, it is usually glossed over, and conveys the writer's preconceived fears and warnings that magick is dangerous, and should only be used as a last resort.

Fear, especially fear of power and the unknown, are natural, and since some of today's Wiccan writers come from Christian backgrounds their fears are understandable—not necessarily reason-able—but understandable. For example, I had a student ask me if it was possible to *accidentally* do a work of black magick. It seems she had read that you must always do divination before you do magick, so you don't "*accidentally*" do black magick. This is absurd. It is not possible to "*accidentally*" do a work of black magick, any more than it is possible to "*accidentally*" commit premeditated first-degree murder. Both actions require malice aforethought and conscious effort on the part of the perpetrator.

I suspect this was an editorial error, and that the author intended it to read "so you don't accidentally make a mistake" rather than "accidentally do black magick." And, even though it is a good idea to do divination prior to planning a magickal rite to confirm that the conditions are favorable, it is not mandatory.

For instance, you want a job promotion. You do your divination and it tells you this is not a good time to ask for a promotion, that you would be better off doing an attraction spell to get your supe-riors' attention. So, you do an attraction ritual. Suddenly your superiors take notice of your work and are made aware of your value to the company. Now you are in a position to do a mag-ickal rite to secure the job promotion—your original goal. As you can see, the process took some planning and effort on your part. This pretty much rules out the possibility of "*accidentally*" doing anything.

Magick is the manipulation of energy—controlling the natural forces that surround us through focused attention. It is a tool or process we, Wiccan witches, use to cause a change to occur in accordance with our will. Magick is not evil, it is not black, it is not white, it is simply energy—energy that we can use to obtain those things we desire, or repel those things that are harmful. It can be used to heal or it can be used to hurt; it all depends on the *intentions* of the person using it. Magick, like energy, feels nothing one way or the other. Its only concern is to get from its point of origin to its point of destination.

Magick is not complicated, without structure, or in opposition to nature. In fact, magick is just the opposite. It brings you into alignment with the natural flow of universal energy. Once your mind and body are in sync with the rhythms of the universe, things just automatically begin to fall into place. By tapping into the powers of nature, through seasonal shifts and lunar transitions, you learn to control your segment of the universe. This control is what allows you to manifest your desires.

Wicca as a religion, and magick as a science, are meant to help people, including yourself. The idea that magick should not be used for personal gain but only to help others, is pure foolishness. If you study the lives of famous Witches and magicians, you find that they lived well and enjoyed the creature comforts of their time. And while magick might not solve all of your problems, it will solve enough of them to make it worth your while.

Wiccan Magick for Beginners

How Magick Works

> "Magick is the science and art of causing change
> to occur in conformity with will."
> —Aleister Crowley, *Magick in Theory and Practice*

Magick is something everyone can do and is only as good or evil as the individual using it. However, because magick is not instantaneous, and works through the invisible world of *thought-forms*, it can only be proved in retrospect. This has caused the often skeptical and scientifically minded community to scoff at its effectiveness. For the rest of us, magick works, and is a constructive way to achieve our goals.

Like any philosophy, magick has infinite possibilities as well as distinct limitations. It relies heavily on the strength of character and mental ability of the individual using it. Probably the most limiting factors in magick are those of fear and frustration. Obstacles such as these are created by lack of knowledge and experience. We only fear what we do not understand.

Frustration and fear are created through lack of experience, but they can be brought under control with training and practice.

However, they can never be totally eliminated because of their relationship to our survival. The key here is that *they can be controlled*.

Magick is one of the best ways to gain control and bring harmony back into your life. It is what unleashes your personal power and rekindles your divine spark. Magick allows you, as an individual, to create or bring into physical reality what you most desire. All anyone needs to make magick work for them is an open mind, some basic understanding of universal principles, and a willingness to experiment.

Magick is a process and a tool that can move or bend reality. It is equivalent to change and our ability to alter reality. Why the emphasis on change? Because nothing ever stays the same! All matter is in a constant state of motion. We need only to look back a few years to see how things have changed. How many of us are still wearing the same clothes we did a year ago? If they have not worn out, they are definitely out of style. The same thing is usually true of our friends, some are still around, some have moved, and new ones have come on the scene. We change jobs, houses, cars, and attitudes. Consciously or unconsciously, we all move with the flow of current trends. What was important to most of us five years ago (more than likely) is less than a memory today.

Magick can help us make changes and aid in solving impossible situations. Regrettably, magick has been kept as a highly guarded secret by those who really understand it. What has managed to surface has been so muddled or intellectually confusing, that most people shrug it off as superstitious nonsense. Consequently, the power and possibilities of this wonderful tool have been either denied or rejected by the vast majority.

Magick is not harmful, sinful, or complicated. It is a tool that can be easily used by anyone wishing to create change. You simply must have the desire to make or change something. Unfortunately, change can be a very frightening thing when one comes face to face with it. We all get used to the way things are, and comfortable with being able to perceive the outcome of our actions. This ability to predict, and therefore deal with the outcome of a situation, ceases when we change the surrounding circumstances.

Just think of how many times you have seen your friends (or even yourself, if you're honest) trapped in an undesirable situation, and you wonder why they don't do something about it. They don't do something to change it, even though the situation at hand is uncomfortable, because at least they know where it is going and are more comfortable with the undesirableness then the unknown that change can bring about. To change this would bring in all sorts of unknown factors, which they might not be able to cope with or control.

Unknown Factors Create Fear

Fear of change, fear of the unknown, or just plain fear keeps many of us locked away in our own personal prisons. Magick can free us from these self-created cells by restoring our self-esteem and confidence. It teaches us sometimes through even minor accomplishments, that we can make changes to our situations and ourselves. Most importantly, magick teaches us that we can do it alone. We have everything we need inside of ourselves, and we just need to learn how to bring it out and use it.

The vast majority of people who get into magick do so secretly, and because of this their accomplishments are their own and not necessarily shared with others. Personal accomplishment is a very important aspect of magick and is the beginning of recognition of personal power. Nothing can replace the inner awareness of "I did it, and I did it all by myself." This is truly an awakening experience for those who have been conditioned to believe they aren't capable of doing anything, let alone getting what they want.

However, as with anything else in life, there are certain rules and principles that govern the movement of magick. These rules are not complex or without reason, they are just good, common sense. Unfortunately, common sense is something we all lack when the "I want it now" mentality takes over. The one differentiating factor with magick, compared to other philosophical or metaphysical applications, is that it will allow your obsession to manifest. Getting what we think we want is sometimes a necessary evil.

We are all here to learn, and learn we do in one way or the other. It is like we never really get out of school. We just graduate from one grade to another. Each "grade" brings with it it's own teachers, lessons, tests, accomplishments, and disappointments. The effort we put into study and research, and then to applying what we have learned, determines our final grade. This is where magick comes in. It makes the learning easier, the lessons more profitable, and the outcome one of our choosing.

How Magick Works

Magick works by removing what is unwanted from our lives, and then filling the space with something that is wanted. Everyone knows that you can have only one object in a space at a time. This is true of both tangible objects as well as intangible ones. Thoughts are the objects of our desires, which manifest as thought-forms, and so take up space. If we get rid of the undesirable thought-forms, then we will have room for the beneficial ones. It is just that simple.

We have all seen successful people and wished we were like them. We can be just by changing our attitudes and taking chances on new and different things. In fact, when you think about it, you can't be sure that the successful people you admire most didn't use magick to get what they now have.

The most important denominator in all magickal operations is the rule of *resolution through frustration*. This means that when all conceivable physical methods of obtaining something have failed, we then enlist the powers of magick. We must exhaust all of the possible ways of getting what we want first. It is the frustration of working for something and not being able to get it that raises the psychic energy level.

Along with the law of resolution through frustration comes another control factor: *the path of least resistance*. This means that magick will travel toward its goal on the most natural, effortless course possible. Magick avoids tipping the scales of fate and Karma that invariably generate a coincidence response. The answers you seek will not literally thump you over the head. They will show as subtle answers, so be aware of possibilities.

For example, for those of you who ritually attempt to conjure up your dream mate, be aware that he or she will not fall from the sky into your arms. More than likely (s)he will bump into you on the street or at your place of work. The winning lottery number will not miraculously appear inscribed upon your wall, though it may surface during a dream. This is all part of the way magick works, it avoids opposition and creates the desired effect. It really doesn't matter in the scheme of things how or why magick works, all that really counts is that it does work, and it brings about the desired result.

Of equal importance is the rule or law of *origination through passion*. This is what will actually bring into manifestation your desires, and is the determining factor of whether or not your magick will work. Do you really need those things that you think you want or think you should have? In other words can you live without what you are lusting after? More than likely you can and have been doing so for a long time. This is important, because actual need will influence the amount of energy you are able to produce at any one given time. This in turn will directly influence the magickal work itself.

The line between need and want is very fine. Often it is difficult, if not downright impossible, to distinguish requirements from indulgences. There is nothing wrong with wanting or acquiring material pleasures as long as perspective is kept. This is one aspect of magick that so many aspiring magicians seem to overlook or disregard.

It seems that humankind has never been able to maintain its equilibrium when it comes to desire verses need. Humans will either totally abstain from all types of physical gratification or indulge their fleshly whims to the point of avarice or greed. Somewhere, in between these two opposites, there is a point of balance where the individual can discover true happiness.

Don't make the mistake of thinking that denial of the physical will bring forth spiritual illumination; in fact just the opposite will occur. Lack of proper nourishment, continued lack of sexual expression, sweat, or goose bumps—do not help to produce enlightenment. These types of abstinences generate unnatural obsessions—obsessions that take their toll and can eventually destroy the true spirit of the individual. The same is true of those who rationalize their extravagances, thinking they can outwit the system. Everyone has to answer for their actions, no matter what their muddled excuse.

It is important to realize early on just how powerful magick can be. There is an old adage that says "Be careful what you ask for, you just may get it." Sometimes what we think we want is not necessarily what we need. The true (higher[1]) self knows what is best and has the unique ability of controlling or rationing out levels of personal energy. This can be very upsetting for those with unyielding passions. If the higher self holds back on the energy level, more than likely the desire will not manifest in its expected form.

The higher self is only interested in the progress and survival of the soul or spirit. As far as it is concerned, everything else is just an arbitrary distraction from its true destiny. However, in order

[1]The True-Higher Self: the part of the individual that is endowed with the urge to create and the urge to return to the perfection from which it came. It is the source of wisdom and knowledge—the divine spark within each individual.

to keep you in balance and from going over the edge, the higher self allows for certain material preoccupations. This is why there will be times when your magick seems to work almost immediately, while on other occasions nothing seems to happen. Results are dependant on the acquisition of energy from the higher self to the lower self. The physical consciousness then changes this energy into usable power. This power is then directed or focused toward the desired goal, which causes the reality of the objective to bend or move in accordance with will.

The entire purpose of magick is to create or cause a change. The key word here is *create*. In order for you to create or change something you must take action. Desire is not enough unless it is backed up by some sort of physical activity. Wishful thinking never changed anything, but action (work) does.

When all is said and done, magick is the most marvelous tool we have at our disposal. It permits us to create or reshape our own personal segment of the universe. Magick, when properly used, allows us the freedom to express our highest aspirations. For within the bounds of ritual magick the individual reigns supreme.

The Language of Magick

When you enter any new field of study, it is a good idea to learn the language used by those in the field. Any situational shift requires a shift in language, which makes it necessary to learn those terms being used to express the intent and significance of the new area of interest. Wicca and magick, as a field of study, are no different. There are very distinctive terms that help communicate the principles, beliefs, and functions of Wicca and magick. For this reason a glossary of terms has been placed here, at the beginning of this book, rather than in the back.

I suggest that you take some time and learn the language of magick. It will not only make your study a whole lot easier, but there really is no way to forge ahead, work magick, and perform rituals, if you don't understand the principles that support them.

10

In addition, having a grasp of the language makes it easier to speak with others. This builds confidence and promotes participation. When we don't fully understand what others are saying, we tend to stand back rather than get involved.

MAGICKALLY SPEAKING

Air   One of the four creative elements in magick. Air corresponds to the East—the direction of new beginnings. It is associated with the mind, inspiration, and intellect. The astrological signs of Air are Aquarius, Gemini, and Libra. Air is blue and represented by a circle.

Altar   A small square or round table used for magickal practice, usually placed in the center of the circle. The altar is where all obeisance is directed and focused during a magickal rite. The altar reflects the personality of the individual using it. Basically, the altar provides the backdrop for ritual, establishes the theme of the magickal work being done, and sets the mood for ceremony.

Amulet   An object left in its virgin state, usually worn as a charm.

Arcana   Derived from *arcanus*, a Latin term meaning "secret of hidden knowledge." It is also used to denote the major and minor cards of the Tarot.

Astral   (Latin *astar*, star) refers to the level of awareness in the etheric world which is close to the mundane world.

Athame   The Witches' double-edged knife that is used to direct personal power during ritual. It is usually about nine inches in length, has a black handle, and is personally consecrated and charged by the Witch for use in magickal rites. The athame is only used symbolically and never to let blood or cut material objects.

Banish   The process of getting rid of unwanted energies that might influence a spell or ritual.

Bind   To psychically constrict or restrain someone magically to do your will.

Blessing Benediction. Laying on of hands to confer personal power, energy, or good will to another person or on a material object.

Book of Shadows A personal journal or diary kept by the Witch and magician that contains all their spells, magickal formulas, and rituals. Traditionally the cover of the book is black with a pentagram inscribed on its cover. Most Wiccans and trained magicians consider their *Book of Shadows* to be their most valuable tool of the art.

Cakes and Wine A sacred meal comprised of small cakes or unleavened bread wafers and wine that is blessed and consecrated during ritual.

Cauldron A large black kettle. The cauldron is a symbol of the Goddess, transmutation, transformation, regeneration, and germination.

Censer Incense burner or heat proof container for burning incense and magickal offerings. The censer is usually placed directly on the altar during magickal rites.

Chalice The Witches' magickal cup. It represents the element of water during magickal rites. It is considered a sacred symbol of the Goddess. The chalice is used for blessing wine and other liquids during ceremonies and ritual acts. It is usually made of silver, or silver lined with gold to emphasize the divine union of opposites.

Chant The use of rhymes, words, and tones for the purpose of raising and directing energy (personal power) toward a desired goal. Also used in meditation to achieve or induce a state or altered states of consciousness.

Charging The act of passing or infusing an object with personal power and energy. The use of chants or tones are employed to focus the attention on the object being charged.

Circle A sphere of magickal energy created by the Witch or magician. The circle is usually marked on the floor physically, and then charged by projecting psychic energy onto its boundary. The circle is a barrier of protection and is used to contain energy raised during magickal rites.

Cone of Power   An invisible, cone shaped body of psychic energy which is raised during specific magickal rites, and is then focused and directed toward an individual or used to achieve a definite purpose. Witches will raise the cone of power to protect their land, heal sick friends, or create material abundance.

Conjuration   This is the act of summoning a spiritual force or energy source.

Consecration   The act of blessing to remove and/or infuse an object with energy. The Witch or magician will always consecrate all his or her magickal tools, and all physical objects that will be used during magickal operations.

Conscious Mind   The place in the brain that manipulates information, such as the environmental stimuli of hearing, seeing, tasting, smelling, feeling, and experiencing. Logical thought, the rational part of our consciousness.

Coven   A group of Witches, usually led by a High Priestess and High Priest. The coven usually consists of thirteen members who meet for working magick on the night of the full moon, and for celebrating the eight seasonal shifts or changes. The **covenstead** is the place Witches meet and is usually the home of the High Priestess or High Priest.

Craft   A modern term used to refer to Wicca or Witchcraft as a magickal system. It is often used in place of the word Wicca or Witchcraft.

Deosil   To move in a clockwise direction, which is considered to be positive. Most Witches will walk deosil when they are within the bounds of their magick circle.

Divination   The act of divining the future. The practice of fortune-telling using symbols such as Tarot cards, dice, tea leaves, Runes, and astrology to foresee future events.

Earth   One of the four creative elements of magick. Earth corresponds to the North—the direction of foundation. It is associated with physical ability, perseverance, experience, and abundance. The astrological signs for Earth are Capricorn, Taurus, and Virgo. Earth is yellow and represented by a square.

East The compass quarter associated with the element of Air.

Elemental A deliberately formed and controlled thought-form of intelligent energy that is capable of performing menial tasks for its master.

Elements Considered to be the four building blocks of life which can be used to enhance magickal works, they are Air, Fire, Water, Earth.

Evocation To summon and or conjure an appearance of spiritual force.

Familiar An elemental, or totem animal such as a cat, that has been programmed to be a magickal servant of the Witch or magician. Once the animal has become a familiar, it will have a special bond with its master.

Fire One of the four creative elements of magick. Fire corresponds to the South—the direction of power. It is associated with energy, passion, and strength. The astrological signs of Fire are Aries, Leo, and Sagittarius. Fire is red and represented by a triangle.

Full Moon The time of the month when the moon is fully visible. The Full Moon is considered to be a time of great power and magickal potential. The Full Moon is associated with the Great Goddess, shapeshifting, fertility, and magick. Most Wiccans meet and practice their craft on the night of the full moon.

Glamour The act of casting a magickal spell on another individual using only personal power. Glamour is the art of fascination or making someone see, believe, and do something they might not ordinarily do or think of.

Great Rite A term for ritual-sexual union. In some traditions this is part of the third-degree initiation. In modern Wicca, the Great Rite is enacted symbolically by the conjoining of the chalice and the athame as a representation of the Goddess (chalice) and God (athame).

Herbs Medicinal plants that have magickal qualities. Herbs are used to make oils, incenses, and brews. They correspond to planetary symbolism and contain magickal and healing properties.

Hex (German, *hexan*, meaning "Witch") A non-Wiccan term used to denote a negative magickal working.

Incantation The act of singing, chanting, or speaking formulaic words, phrases, or sounds to raise energy for manipulation during spell casting and ritual magick.

Incense A fragrant mixture of resins, herbs, and oils that is used in magickal and ritual work. It is believed that prayers and words of power can be carried on the smoke of magickally charged incense.

Initiation The ceremony by which an individual is welcomed into the ranks of the Wiccan priesthood. During the ceremony, the person is transformed and realigned with deity, and he or she is reborn into the Wiccan mysteries.

Invocation (Latin, *invocatia* meaning "to call upon") The act of calling down or summoning of a God force to aid the Witch or magician in their work. The act of invocation psychically links or binds the individual with the force to aid in the performance of psychic feats.

Karma The metaphysical law of cause and effect, action and reaction. Karma is the "great equalizer." It does not reward or punish, but is simply a law that reacts to causation until disharmony is resolved.

Libation The practice of pouring wine or other blessed liquid on the ground in honor of deity.

Linking The process of using mental identification to communicate with spiritual forces and/or with appropriate symbols in a magickal operation.

Magick (Greek, Zoroaster *magein*, meaning "great; the great science and religion") A system of concepts and methods of using the subtle forces of nature to help the individual alter reality; to cause change to occur in accordance with will; the art and ability to manifest desire through an intricate system of symbols, ritual, and spell work.

Magnetism Magickal power, life force. The energy projected by the Witch or magician that influences his or her immediate surroundings.

Mighty Ones A term for the Guardians of the Quadrants, Archangels, or Divine Emanations that are evoked prior to religious or magickal rites.

Mystery Tradition Any mystical or magickal order that uses initiation to pass on its secret teachings.

North The compass quarter associated with the element of Earth.

Occult (Latin, *occultusanum*, meaning "secret" or "hidden") The meaning of this word basically hasn't changed through time. However, it was only after the onset of Christianity that the word "occult" took on a sinister meaning.

Oil Scented oils that have been aligned with planetary forces and magnetized during ritual are used for anointing candles, objects, and individuals during magickal rites.

Pentacle A round disk of wood or stone that is inscribed with a five-pointed star. In Wicca and magick, the pentacle represents the element of Earth, and is often used as the focal point of magickal rites. Objects can be placed on the pentacle to charge, or to symbolize an objective.

Pentagram A five-pointed star image with interlaced lines that is usually enclosed within a circle. The pentagram symbolizes the spirit (the top point of the star), in control of four elements of nature and human awareness (Air, Fire, Water, Earth). Pentagrams can be found in decorative motifs, and have been used since the early 1700s in Freemasonary.

Philtre   A magickal potion used in love spells and other types of enchantment.

Poppets   Small handmade dolls used in spells and magick. The poppet is made in the likeness of the person on whom the spell is being performed. The theory is that whatever happens to the poppet will in turn happen to the person the poppet represents.

Psychic Awareness   The sensitivity of the body and mind to subtle vibrations usually emanating from the astral plane or from another human being.

Qabalah (also spelled Cabala, Kabala, Kabalah)   A complex system of Hebrew magick. The Qabalah is considered to be a blueprint of creation and the inner workings of Divine consciousness.

Rede   A code of conduct. The Wiccan Rede is considered to be the cornerstone of modern Wicca, stating, "and ye harm none, do what thou wilt."

Ritual   A prescribed event, or a particular form of ceremony that is built up by tradition through repetitious activity. Rituals are performed to celebrate the night of the full moon, the traditional eight Sabbats, and, and for set times of magickal operations.

Sabbat   A Witches religious festival celebrated eight times a year. The Sabbats occur on October 31 (Samhain), December 21 (Yule), February 1 (Imbolc), March 21 (Ostara), April 30 (Beltane), June 21 (Litha), August 1 (Lughnasadh), and September 21 (Mabon).

Salt   Salt has always been considered a purifying agent. In Wiccan rites it is used to cleanse and purify the area in which the ritual or magickal rite will be held. Traditionally, salt is placed in a bowl on the altar and represents the element of Earth.

Sigil   A magickal seal usually comprised of a set of lines, numbers or symbolic figures and usually inscribed on parchment paper, metal, wood, or other natural substance.

Skull   A symbol of knowledge and wisdom, and link to the spirit and other world.

Spell　A period of time during which a person or object is held captive by another person for the benefit of the person working the spell. A word, words, chant, or music that have a dominating influence over another individual. In modern Wicca, a spell is a simple basic act of magick that focuses the power of the mind to cause a change to occur in accordance with the will of the individual working the spell.

Symbol　Things that imply more than their obvious and immediate meaning. In magick, symbols are considered to be agents of power that bind together designator and designated in some association or remembrance.

Talisman　An object that has been consecrated and is believed to contain magickal powers.

Tarot　A system of divination using seventy-eight symbolic cards that represent phases of life and the human condition.

Thought-forms　Different shapes of ethereal substance, defined or cloudy, large or small, varying in color and density that float through space or hover over persons' heads. They are capable of being perceived clairvoyantly. Also ergs of energy emanating from the head area that are charged with degrees of intelligence and emotion, and occupy their position in space according to their disposition. When a thought-form is created magickally, it will solidify and eventually manifest on the physical plane.

Visualization　The process of making thought-forms or forming mental images to enhance magickal work and spell crafting. The ability to recreate an image once seen within the mind. Total recall.

Wand　The second, and most valued of the four major working tools of the Witch. It is symbolic of the Air element, and is used for directing energy. The wand is phallic in shape and represents the will of the Witch or magician. It is usually the length of an individual's arm from the tip of the middle finger to the inside of the elbow.

Waning   A term used to denote loss or decrease, as in the waning (decreasing in size) of the moon.

Water   One of the four elements in magick. Water corresponds to the West—the direction of psychic ability. It is associated with regeneration, intuition, and emotion. The astrological signs of Water are Cancer, Scorpio, Pisces. Water is green and represented by a crescent.

Waxing   A term used to denote gain or increase, as in the waxing (increasing in size) of the moon.

Wheel of the Year   A term for the seasons of the year. The cycles of nature turn like a wheel, waxing and waning from the first blossom of spring to the last harvest in the fall. The wheel denotes birth, life, death, and return.

Wicca   A current and more popular name for Witchcraft. A Neo-Pagan religion that expresses a reverence for nature, a polytheistic view of deity, and practices simple ceremonies to achieve communion with the natural forces of Mother Earth.

Widdershins   The term used to denote the counter-clockwise motion within a ritual circle.

Wine   A symbol of the life-giving essence of blood. In matriarchal times, the wine represented the power of the of the Goddess to bring forth life. In patriarchal times, the wine was a symbol of the slain God.

Working   A term used to describe a magickal act: The process the Witch or magician uses to reach a specific state of mind that will create a desired effect to manifest a goal.

Zodiac   An invisible band in the sky in which the planets are perceived to move within. The placement of the planets has a direct effect on the life and nature of earth. By knowing the location of a specific planet, the individual is able to divine future events. There are twelve places, or houses, in which the planets reside at different times of the year.

3

The Four Elements of Wiccan Magick

"Nature, as a whole and in all its elements, enunciates
something that may be regarded as an indirect self-
communication of God to all those ready to receive it."
—Martin Buber, *At the Turning*

The world we live in is a combination of a multitude of forces
all working together to maintain life. These forces are comprised of both physical (chemical) and metaphysical (spiritual)
elements that are fundamental to the creation process and essential for supporting life as we know it. Knowledge of these principle
forces is necessary if we are to understand ourselves, the universe,
and the dynamic energy that controls it.

These principle forces are the four basic elements of Air, Fire,
Water, and Earth. These elements are the underlying principles
which are responsible for the structure of this world and other
basic phenomena. In general, most Wiccan, Pagan, and metaphysical philosophies consider these elements to be symbolic rep-

resentations of potential energy that radiates from deities as well as from various archetypal sources.

To our ancestors, who were responsible for creating and developing the early magickal–religious systems, these natural constituents were considered to be both a power unto themselves as well as an emanation from deity. It was sensed that alignment with these natural forces would automatically render most gods and goddesses vulnerable to humans needs and desires. This is why mankind devised different ways to use his surroundings in the honor and worship of deity.

Mankind first enlisted the powers of nature through his hunting rituals. These rituals employed a horned god, whose nature was in harmony with the animals, for assistance during the hunt. By acting out the hunt in front of a drawing or image of the god, the god would surely take notice and protect the men from danger as well as provide them with a successful hunt.

Another way of awakening the gods to man's needs was through the powers of early fertility rites. It was through the sexual act during ritual that the atmosphere was stimulated with human energy, this would in turn motivate the gods to quicken the propagation of the herd or increase the harvest yield.

Generally, most people will agree on the existence of the four primordial elements, even though today we know there are many more which make up the world of matter. Philosophically and symbolically the four elements, Air, Fire, Water, and Earth still remain as the primary focus of power and energy in most New Age and magickal religious systems. These elements are believed to be universal principles, which when understood, controlled, and arranged in a specific order, help the individual devise a more perfect reality.

The elements are one of the essential building blocks of nature and serve to create a framework in which energy, emotion and expression can be defined. The use of these forces is paramount to creating a spiritual system in which you can function and work to your optimum.

Learning about the elements and the areas of your life they control is an important step in your spiritual development. Once you begin to harmonize with these magickal forces of nature you become privilege to their knowledge and wisdom. The insight you gain from interacting with the elements will help balance your thinking and emotions. This is important because it is very difficult to be spiritual if you are overwhelmed with passion, inflamed with anger or given to flights of fancy.

Besides being good for controlling emotions, the elements are associated with almost everything we come in contact with. They correspond to the seasons, different times of the day and night, even to plants, stones and places. Astrologically they provide the data which makes it possible to understand different personality types and modes of expression. Without a doubt the elements are one of natures greatest contributions. They are a wondrous storehouse of knowledge just waiting to be tapped into.

AIR, FIRE, WATER, EARTH

AIR

Air is thought to be a subtle material realm between the physical and spiritual plane. Air speaks to the intellect and brings forth the true essence of the individual through the creative imagination. The element of air represents new beginnings, the thought process and creativity.

Air has always been associated with breath which is synonymous with the "spirit" or "soul" of all living creatures. The idea of air or breath giving life to the soul or spirit dates back to the time of matriarchal rule. For it was the women after giving birth who would gently breathe[1] into her child's mouth initiating the breathing process. In Greece the female air soul was Pneuma which

---

[1] As with a lot of things this act of gently breathing into the newborn's mouth was eventually replaced with the patriarchal slap on the buttocks to expel evil and sin.

Air Qualities, Associations, and Correspondences

Aquarius, Gemini, and Libra are the three astrological Air signs. The principle concern of Air people is that of "communication." People with a predominance of air think, communicate, analyze and theorize. They love freedom, and truth and have a strong sense of justice and fair play. Air people have the ability to change circumstances with amazing speed, they are like cats, and usually land on their feet.

The devotion to abstract ideas, and the hard time Air people have making commitments can make them seem elusive as well as exasperating at times. They are thinkers, and rely on rationality, rather than on emotion to confront a situation. They can tolerate almost any circumstance as long as there is a rational explanation for it.

Spiritually Air comes from the East on the wings of the Archangel Raphael whose name means "healer of God." One of this magnificent creature's abilities is to heal both the physical body and well as the spirit. He is usually depicted with a bow and arrow and a crystal vial of healing balm.

COLOR:	Blue, silver, white, gray
SYMBOLS:	Circle, bird, bell, sylph, flute, chimes, clouds
TOOLS:	Wand, rod, staff
PLANTS:	Almond, broom, clover, eyebright, lavender, pine
STONES:	Amethyst, sapphire, citrine, azurite
PLACES:	Sky, mountain tops, tree tops, bluffs, airplanes
ZODIAC:	Aquarius, Gemini, Libra
TIME:	Spring, dawn
ARCHANGEL:	Raphael
DIRECTION:	East
PROCESS:	Thinking, reading, speaking, praying, singing

means "breath" or the Muse who always brought inspiration, giving poets and seers the power of understanding.

Breathing is paramount to life itself. Breath enters our bodies at birth and withdraws at death. It has long been believed that the soul or spirit leaves the body at death on the breath of the person. It was for this reason, in the past, that mirrors were held close to the mouth of a dying person in hopes of capturing their soul in the mirror. This belief came about through old folklore which spoke of mirrors as being soul traps, and the realm of the dead as being the Hall of Mirrors.

Air is the bridge between spiritual inspiration and the conscious projection of ideas. Fresh clean air is exhilarating, it is movement, and it inspires creativity. Air is feminine, innovation and the ability to conceive of new ways and approaches to do things. Air is the tie that binds us together through conversation, intellectual sharing and the endless seeking of knowledge.

FIRE

Fire is transformation; the life-giving generative powers of the sun. It is emblematic of the masculine deity in many cultures and is the element of fervent intensity, aspiration and personal power. Fire is the force which motivates and drives all living organisms. Fire along with air creates energy, gets us going and produces stamina. "What the mind can imagine (air), the will (fire) can create".

Fire is bright, brilliant and flamboyant and unfortunately neither stable or logical. Fire leaps intuitively to grasp the moment with little regard for what is around it. Fire is reckless, seeking and passionate and knows only itself. Fire is unique because in order for it to create it must first consume or destroy. This concept is plainly exhibited in the forest fire. The fire burns, consumes and destroys the trees and underbrush of the forest which in time will produce new growth. Fire is the active element within all of us. Fire pushes towards the new by getting rid of the old.

Fire Qualities, Associations, and Correspondences

The astrological signs for Fire are Aries, Leo and Sagittarius. The best way to describe a Fire person is "they are the essence of passion." When I use the word passion I don't just mean sexual desire but rather all powerful emotions. Most fire people have intense appetites for living life to the fullest. They experience love, hate, anger, enthusiasm, desire, pain and death all with extreme intensity.

To the fire person everything is intense and when nothing is happening they will create something, even if what they create causes trouble for them. They are seekers of passion, and are willing to suffer for it in order to avoid boredom.

The mind of the Fire person is quick and active and most people find them attractive if not a little dangerous at times—they just like the fire in the hearth on a cold day. With an emphasis on having an adventure, and a vivid experience, the Fire person often hurts others in the process. The problem is they are so blinded by their own desires they respond without consideration for those around them.

The element of fire is spiritually brought to us by the supreme commander of the armies of Light, Michael. This illuminating agent of Divine Light, whose name means "Perfect of God" is the guardian of the southern quarter. He is visualized as a Roman soldier dressed in red and gold and ready to do battle against all evil.

COLOR:	Red, red-orange (as in flames), amber
SYMBOLS:	Triangle, lightning, flame, salamander
TOOLS:	Sword, dagger, fire pot, double-headed ax
PLANTS:	Basil, blood root, Dragons Blood, orange, tobacco
STONES:	Ruby, garnet, diamond, bloodstone, flint, sunstone˙
PLACES:	Volcanoes, ovens, fire places, deserts,
ZODIAC:	Aries, Leo, Sagittarius
ARCHANGEL:	Michael
TIME:	Summer, noon
DIRECTION:	South
PROCESS:	Passion, anger, quick, active, energy, power

For fire to be used constructively it must first be contained. When fire is contained its energy can be used and directed towards a desired purpose, such as heat or light. It is the same way with the personal forces it dominates such as passion, anger and aggression. When these emotions are controlled and their energy channeled in a constructive manner, they bring about positive reconstruction. Everyone knows what happens when these feelings go unchecked, just like fire, they wreck havoc, bring destruction and create chaos.

The element of fire is spiritually brought to us by the supreme commander of the armies of Light, Michael. This illuminating agent of Divine Light, whose name means "Perfect of God" is the guardian of the southern quarter. He is visualized as a Roman soldier dressed in red and gold and ready to do battle against all evil.

WATER

Water is the third basic element and the most primary form in which liquid can exist. Water is passive, receptive, and the source of all potentialities in existence. It is associated with the Great Mother, the universal womb, birth and fertility. Water is emblematic of the life giving and life destroying abilities of the universe. Water is used to cleanse or purify physically as well as psychically. Where air is the intellect, fire the energy and drive, water is the emotional response to situations—fluid, sensitive, and giving. When heated by passion, water brings forth life, but when cooled by indifference, death results. This is why so many religions use immersion in water to symbolize the return to a primordial state of purity. In essence the baptism or dunking of an individual in water signifies death and rebirth of both body and the spirit.

The element of Water is both detached and willful as it flows freely. However there are times when Water will allow itself to be contained. Water is a gentle element and it inspires intuition and the desire to worship. The element of Water is truly linked to and

Water Qualities, Associations, and Correspondences

The astrological signs for Water are Cancer, Scorpio and Pisces. These people are sensitive, aware of the feelings of others, and generally in tune with their surroundings on an emotional level. They just naturally sense the vibration of the Universe and the mythic meaning behind reality.

Water people live in a spiritual world and have an affinity for nature and healing. They are usually very loving of the world around them, and sometimes find it hard to draw a line between those things they should care about and those they should leave alone.

The major problem the Water person faces is sensitivity which can cause them to break under the stress of just "feeling too much." This can lead to escape through drugs or other addictions as well as cause them to be unforgiving and hold on to old hurts. Water can flow with love bringing green pastures in its wake or gouge and eat away at the landscape through flooding until nothing is left.

Gabriel is the Archangel of the West, the spiritual aspect of water and the one who is destined to "Sound the last trumpet." Gabriel, like water, is fertility in all its forms. His role is that of initiator of physical life and he is pictured holding the Grail as he emerges from the sea of immortality.

COLOR:	Green, turquoise
SYMBOLS:	Crescent, shells, boats, ship wheel, anchor, cup
TOOLS:	Vessel, grail, chalice, cauldron
PLANTS:	Aloe, cucumber, dulse, gardenia, lily, lotus, willow
STONES:	Aquamarine, chrysocolla, moonstone, mother-of-pearl,
PLACES:	Ocean, river, lakes, ponds, waterfalls, beaches
ZODIAC:	Cancer, Scorpio, Pisces
ARCHANGEL	Gabriel
TIME:	Autumn, sunset
DIRECTION:	West
PROCESS:	Love, nurture, sensitivity, psychic ability, healing

part of the Goddess which is within all of us. Water is remembering the past and foreseeing the future. As water brings life it can also bring destruction, the key factor is in governing its energy.

EARTH

Earth has the vibrational frequency that forms a solid quality, is considered to be passive in nature and negative in polarity. The earth symbolically represents both the womb and the grave; that which brings life forth and that which takes it away or reclaims it. However, unlike water the earth is stationary and does not actively create. The earth is seen mystically as the final outcome. It provides the other three elements with a place to physically make manifest a desire. Earth is our base of operation where we exhibit the final product of our imagination.

Earth is related to physical matter and the world of corporal reality. It is all we can see, touch, smell and feel, the sensual and practical side of life. Earth is both stubborn as well as generous— slow and steady ever changing while remaining the same.

No matter who you are or where you live, the elements in some way or another affect your life. The elements are everywhere; you cannot avoid their influence. However, there are ways to work with them so they balance within the mind and body. Reaching balance and a point of mental and physical equilibrium is necessary if you are going to be effective, especially magickally.

The simplest and most effective way of achieving balance in your life is by recognizing your dominate and passive elemental qualities. I suggest having your astrological natal chart calculated and interpreted. The chart will provide you with information on important personality qualities and indicate those areas in which you excel. A well calculated natal chart is a valuable mirror of your true self and can provide you with directional advice in all areas of your life.

I also suggest that you try working with the elements to reawaken your connection to the natural world—where everything is possi-

Earth Qualities, Associations, and Correspondences

The astrological signs for Earth are Taurus, Virgo, and Capricorn, signs associated with the essential qualities of strength, steadfastness, and material gain.

Most Earth people are practical and like organization. They are slow, steady, and solid in their efforts. Earth people have a strong sense of responsibility, and see themselves as builders and defenders.

The Earth signs are concerned with reality and the constants of home, family and work. They are sensual, and like things they can touch, feel, smell, and see in addition to those things they can buy or sell. Earth people rarely get into fads or trends, and tend to be conservative in their approach to life. Earth people are kind, but cautious. It can take years to win their trust and friendship, but once you have it they are loyal forever—they hold on to what they have with a bulldog determination.

Auriel is the Archangel for the element of Earth. He brings the awareness of the Gods as manifested in the beauty of creation. In short, as we behold the wonders of nature we are driven to consider the even greater splendor of the forces which originated it. This Archangel operates at levels beyond that of physical sight and teaches a sense of "cosmic rightness." Auriel bears a glowing lantern in his left hand and a pair of scales in his right.

COLOR:	Yellow, brown, russet
SYMBOLS:	Square, cornucopia, spindle, scythe, salt
TOOLS:	Shield, pentacle, flail, horn,
PLANTS:	Alfalfa, cotton, oats, patchouly, vetivert, wheat
STONES:	Moss agate, jasper, malachite, peridot, tourmaline
PLACES:	Caves, forests, fields, gardens, canyons
ZODIAC:	Capricorn, Taurus, Virgo
ARCHANGEL	Auriel
TIME:	Midnight, winter
DIRECTION:	North
PROCESS:	Responsible, practical, organized, steady, grounded

ble. Take time to breathe and call upon the potential of Air to activate your imagination and inspire new thoughts. Force yourself to act on new ideas, kindle the fire within for added strength and awareness. Learn to control the forces of water and your emotions. Once you are in control of your physical world the earth will provide you the ability to manifest your desires.

An Elemental Spell for Success

Items Needed: four votive candles, one each of blue, red, green, and yellow; sandalwood incense; pen and paper.

On the piece of paper write down one thing you would like to accomplish. Keep it simple and straightforward. Place the paper in front of you and think about what you want. Now place the candles next to the paper at their corresponding points—Blue, East (right-hand side); Red, South (bottom edge); Green, West (left-hand side); Yellow, North (top edge). Take a few moments to relax and to focus your attention on your desire. Light the candles, one at a time, beginning with the Blue in the East and proceeding in a clockwise manner. As soon as you light the North candle slowly begin to chant:

> *Air, Fire, Water, Earth*
> *To my dreams give birth.*

Continue the chant for several minutes. Concentrate on the chant and your voice. Allow the chant to peak and then stop. Relax. Leave the candles to burn for one hour and then extinguish them. Repeat the spell for one week. On the last day of the spell leave the candles to burn out. Bury the paper and forget about the spell. As soon as you let go of the *thought-form* that was created during the spell it will manifest your desire.

4

The Symbolic Tools of Wiccan Magick

"The Symbol expresses or crystallizes some aspect
or direct experience of life and truth,
and thus leads beyond itself."

—J. C. Cooper, *Traditional Symbols*

Every society, philosophy, or religion has its own unique language which expresses its purpose. Wicca and the magickal arts are no different. They have very distinctive symbols, methods of operation, and fundamental principles that communicate their objectives. Once you have an understanding of this special language, the beliefs and practices of Wicca automatically begin to work for you.

The language of magick is a symbolic one; intuitively understood within rather than verbalized. A language that began at the dawn of time, when humanity's ability to create was expressed through its symbols. Even now symbols silently speak to the spirit, intellect, and emotions creating an everlasting impression. It is through the integration of symbols and abstract concepts that we tap into the cosmic consciousness, expand our awareness of the universe, and cause change to occur in accordance with will.

Symbols were (and still are) essential to our thinking. They add quality and meaning to that which surrounds us. They are the fabric from which we form a fundamental understanding of life and our relationship to the universe.

Symbols surround us and speak to our minds without words. The red octagon shaped sign at the end of the road tells us to stop; the green arrow on the light tells us to go. The cigarette in a circle with a line across its face lets us know smoking is not allowed, while a simple drawing of a man or woman on a door indicates the intended gender occupancy of a bathroom.

Similarly, magickal symbols speak to our higher consciousness and enable us to act without effort or work to process information. This is a crucial concept, *for it is during the conversion process that energy and power are at their peak.* The time between absorption and transformation is when projection of desire occurs, and this must be accurate and spontaneous. There can be no break or interruption in the flow of the energy being focused, if there is the results will be corrupted.

The entire process is very simple. In order for your higher self (the mind) to be creative it must be allowed interference-free space. One of the few times the higher self is allowed this special moment is during a ritual when the conscious mind is distracted, and inner dialogue is quieted, During this time actions become mechanical (instinctive) and the higher self is allowed its all important freedom to create, rather than just manipulate what already exists.

Magickally, symbols represent actions, desires and results to both the higher self, and the conscious-physical mind. When we allow a symbol to take over and represent an idea, our conscious mind is expanded, creative energy is focused, and our desires are put into motion.

All symbols have a certain amount of power and in some way connect us to that which they represent. In turn, the energy we force through this connection will affect what resides on the opposite end. A good example of this would be blowing through a straw. Whatever is in the path of the air flow, coming out the opposite end, will be forced to move. Energy always affects or changes that with which it comes in contact.

During an act of magick the symbol being used to represent our request acts like the straw. It directs personal energy towards a goal. What actually happens is the higher consciousness is being projected through the symbolic object, which then changes it to determine the final objective or result. Symbols are the connective link between mundane consciousness, the creative spirit, and manifestation of desire—symbols force mental images onto the material plane.

Wiccan magick, unlike some metaphysical philosophies, actually incorporates the use of physical symbols and tools into its mystical rites and practices. Without effort, Wiccan tools and symbols aid in rasing levels of consciousness, and most importantly they extend personal power beyond the scope of corporeal identity. They elicit an automatic reaction within the mind and assist with the channeling of creative energy toward a specific goal.

It is this drawing from within, then projecting outward, that allows us to manifest our desires. However, in order to make things happen the way we want them to, we must first know how to properly use the symbolic representations of physical-plane images. In other words, we need to learn how to use these special symbols and tools. Then we can create the thought-forms that will direct our energy toward our goals, and bring our dreams into reality.

In the practice of Wiccan magick there are five major symbolic tools that represent the five elements of life—Spirit, Air, Fire, Water, Earth. When each tool is placed within its element it takes on the power and potential of that element. When the tools are aligned with a universal symbol, like that of the pentagram, they

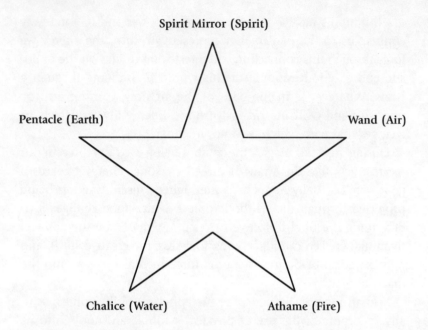

create a powerful circle or conduit of cosmic energy. This energy is then used to create change in accordance with will.

The Spirit mirror represents the astral plane, the divine creation process. As an idea is formulated it is channeled through the air into the mind, represented by the wand. It then is energized by fire, represented by the athame, and becomes the seed of hope. This seed is then nurtured by the symbolic waters of life within the womb or chalice. In time, what was once just a seedling of thought becomes reality, manifested onto the material or earth plane symbolized by the pentacle.

THE PRIMARY TOOLS OF WICCAN MAGICK

THE WAND

A phallic, tubular shaped object that allows your intellectual-psychic energy to be channeled towards a desired objective. By virtue of its shape alone it is masculine in nature. During ritual the wand becomes an extension of the individual using it. Personal power is then forced, with a laser-like intensity, towards the desired goal.

There is a great deal of dispute over whether the wand should be connected with air or fire. From my point of view, and for magickal reasons, the wand is strictly an instrument of the air element. This is one reason our ancestors made their wands from young tree branches. The fresh growth was not only indicative of Spring and the seasons to come, but represented the concept of new beginnings. An important point to note here is, "Time honored tradition contains power." The entire process of first cause, inception, origination and progenitor are ingrained within the symbology of the wand, making it a tool of mind.

The element of air is intellect and provides the environment where abstract thoughts originate. These thoughts enter our consciousness when our creative higher self initiates the manifestation process. This inner communication is one of the keys to magickal success. No amount of wonderful ideas will do us any good if we cannot get them out and make them real. The single most important act in magick is personal dialogue, which produces the realization of desire. This is then coupled with the act of formulation to produce tangible results.

Both symbolically and physically the wand is best suited to the purpose of magickal creation. What happens is, you formulate an idea and then you bring it down into your active consciousness. Once you have a clear picture of what you want, you force all of your attention in that direction. This is done by projecting the flow of personal energy to a specific target area. The "target area" is a symbolic representation of the desired outcome and the wand acts like a laser, directing the flow of power from you to its destination.

Even though this is all symbolic, it is none the less real. Thought is energy and takes up space. Therefore, it is only reasonable to assume if you force another energy into an already occupied space what is there must move or change. This is what magick does best, change, move, or replace what is unwanted with what is desired.

Wands are easy to make. A small branch with a crystal or favorite rock attached, wrapped in leather, works nicely. A simple copper tube with crystals, amethyst or rose quartz connected to the ends produces a wonderful energy conductor. Brass tubing found in most craft shops has all sorts of possibilities, even wooden dowels from a lumber store can, with some imagination, be turned into elegant wands.

My personal wand is made from copper tubing; is eleven inches long and has a rose quartz on one end and an amethyst on the other. Connecting the ends is silver solder spiraled down the shaft. On this there are four stones: garnet, rhodocrosite, gem silica, and lapis. Because of the magickal properties associated with these particular gems this combination helps to balance power through self love and spiritual insight.

Whether you make or buy a wand, the decision is yours. There are many who will insist that all magickal tools should be constructed by the individual using them. This is a wonderful sentiment for those who have the time, equipment and are artistically inclined. For some this is not only unrealistic but impossible. The most important consideration when making or choosing a magickal tool is, how does it feel to you? Will this be something you can relate to and work with? Remember, in magick you are in control, you are the power, and you make all the decisions which affect your life.

THE ATHAME

A double edged knife that represents the element of fire—the masculine, positive force of nature. The athame is associated with fire

because it is the action of fire on iron which produces the end product. Prior to iron smelting, knives were fashioned from flint, which, when rubbed with another piece of flint, would produce a spark. In either case the element of fire is involved, leaving an indelible impression of its essential masculine quality upon the blade.

Fire has always been considered a representation of force, strength and will, so too is its symbolic tool, the sword. Here we are able to see in physical form just what power can do.

Throughout history many myths have been written about the young hero who wields a magickal weapon, coming to the rescue of lady, land and ideal. Probably the best known is Excalibur, the mighty sword of King Arthur given him by the Lady of the Lake. As long as Arthur was in possession of the sword he was invincible. Truth or fiction, it matters not, the symbology of the sword remains the only consideration.

Athames, like wands, come in all shapes, sizes and designs. In the Western hemisphere we see them as being straight and phallic in shape. To the practitioner of Eastern philosophies they are curved and feminine in their appearance. This is due to their legends depicting women as being powerful because of their hold over the life processes. However, in Wicca the athame, as the sword, remains as our Western legends have conditioned us to perceive it—straight and phallic in expression.

The athame, similar to the wand, is used for directing personal power. It helps to focus energy in a desired direction for a specific purpose—it regulates as well as conducts the flow of internal expression towards a desired destination.

With so much emphasis placed on tools in the practice of magick it becomes imperative to remember it is not the objects themselves which are of great consequence, but rather what they represent. "Tools are only symbols and they serve to direct energy toward a desired goal."

THE CHALICE

Also called cup or cauldron, represents the watery realm of our beginnings. It is feminine in nature and represents our emotions and capacity to nurture. Properly embraced emotions keep us in balance. However, unbridled passion can, and usually does, create havoc and dissipates energy.

In order to fully appreciate and avail ourselves of the benefit of the water element, it must first be confined or contained within a suitable vessel. For most magickal works the chalice serves in this capacity to represent the feminine watery side of nature.

As with the athame, there have been countless stories told about beautiful chalices, as well as magickal cauldrons. Arthur and his knights in search of the Grail; the Cauldron of Cerridwen with its regenerative powers; and of course the Witches of MacBeth stirring the cauldron with their bubbling brew of sordid ingredients. These tales serve as examples of how we try to bring into reality and dominate the substance of emotional consciousness.

There is very little, if any, dispute over the symbolic representation of the chalice or cauldron. It is by design alone emblematic of the womb, the Mother Goddess, and the ability to regenerate. This probably accounts for its presence in so many ancient Egyptian, Babylonian and even Christian temples, as it was through the process of spiritual rebirth that an individual gained wisdom, inspiration and enlightenment.

Another aspect to the water element and corresponding symbolic imagery is the challenge or quest factor. Seeking to discover the hidden mysteries of life and death early man took to the sea. Thinking the earth flat, he would surely drop off into the great void were he to sail far enough. What astonishment must have met his eyes when he found others like himself rather than the edge of the universe which he feared. But the quest itself to find and touch his creator far outweighed his fear of death, needless to mention the challenge of hopeful return.

This is where a chalice, like the Grail, fits into magick. It contains the mystery, the hope and promise, of that which is attained when all has been set to rest. It is at once open to observation, while only the surface of what it contains can be seen. One needs to delve deeply within to truly discover what secrets it holds. The emotional factor of that which is yet unknown, will in itself create a powerful energy flow.

THE PENTACLE

The pentacle is not so much a tool as it is the representation of man's ability to create, or manifest an idea. It is the pentacle that helps the magician conceptualize his or her thoughts, with the belief that what is inwardly desired or seen in the mind's eye will  be realized in physical form. The pentacle becomes the point of focus, much like the center of a stage during a play, where all his attention is directed. It is this momentary address of energy towards a single purpose that brings results.

Similar to the chalice, the disk represents the renewal or regeneration of life, and is considered to be feminine in its nature. However, this is from a more brooding, generative, dualistic sense; insofar as it is at the same time both protective and death-dealing like the shield from where it originated. This is brought out clearly in many of the old myths and legends. We see the Knights of the Round Table with their shields (representing their family, life ties) as they go into battle. The shield would protect them from the death-dealing blows of their adversaries; at the same time allowing them to strike back and possibly kill their foe.

The beauty of the pentacle is its versatility. It provides the practitioner of magick, like a canvas for an artist, with a mode of expression. As an individual you can place on the face of the disk or shield any number of unique, symbolic designs. This will represent, to your higher consciousness, an idea in picture form of what you wish to achieve.

For example, you could place the logo of a magickal order upon the face of a pentacle and each time it is used in ritual, the energy that is raised and focused toward the disk would be going for the good of the group as a whole. This is how symbols help us achieve what we want. They force personal power in a specific direction rather than allowing it to scatter and dissipate. With each use of a tool the more distinct the energy becomes. By directing our thoughts through the wand and onto the disk we refine our energy to a considerable extent.

THE SPIRIT MIRROR

The spirit mirror represents wisdom, the mind, higher self, and the soul—the mirror of the universe—a reflection of the super-

natural and Divine intelligence. The mirror is naturally magickal and signifies truth as well as self-knowledge. In magick the mirror is seen as a gateway between the worlds and is generally used as a doorway to the astral plane or for transmitting and receiving communications.

As a reflection of the supernatural and divine intelligence the mirror represents both the sun—and the ability to create, and the moon—reflected light. It symbolizes the mind of the sage, and the ability to look into one's own nature.

Historically, magickal mirrors were used to divine the future. A devotee of the goddess Demeter gazed into a sacred spring and predicted the harvest. It is believed that Catherine de Médicis, a reputed Witch, depended on mirror divination to guide her through the tangled affairs of state in sixteenth century France. And, the *Grimorium Verum*, published in 1517, includes directions for divining by the Mirror of Solomon.

In addition to the five major tools just discussed, there are four secondary tools that are usually required when performing Wiccan rites. Just like the wand, athame, chalice, and pentacle, these secondary tools are associated with the elements.

THE CENSER/THURIBLE OR INCENSE BURNER

This is used in conjunction with the wand to represent the element of Air. It is has long been believed that prayers, and wishes, are delivered to the Gods by way of incense smoke. For this reason, herbal offerings and petitions are often burnt in the censer to aid in love, prosperity and success spells.

THE ELEMENT BOWLS

These are two small bowls or cups set on the altar. One of the bowls contains the element of salt, and the other bowl contains the element of Water. During the opening of most rituals and magickal rites these elements are used to bless and consecrate sacred space, symbolic tools, and even those participating in the rite.

THE ROBE

This is considered by some Witches to be an optional item. However, I believe it plays an important role in creating the proper atmosphere for ritual. Just by putting on your robe you automatically switch from the world of mundane activity to the realm of spiritual expression. It is best if the robe is made from dark colored material so as not to be distracting during ritual. The style and design of the robe should allow for freedom of movement, and not present a hazard when working with candles.

The Book of Shadows

A personal journal in which Witches and magicians write their invocations, rituals, and spells. Its name comes to us from the distant past when magickal journals were penned in secrecy, beneath the veil of night, and contained mysteries of the shadowy Other World. Because its pages were full of secret formulas, and strange incantations, it was believed that if you possessed a Book of Shadows, you possessed the key that would unlock the secrets of the universe.

The Book of Shadows, like any journal, is a collection of personal thoughts and deeds. It will contain information about drying herbs, observing lunar transitions, and instructions for casting spells to attract love, money, and good health. For the most part, it is an accumulation of your magickal practices that you don't want to forget.

The Art of Ritual

"The most important part of any ritual is its intention.
It is simply no use at all to get everything together, and
then try to decide what you are going to do with it all."
—Dolores Ashcroft-Norwicki, *First Steps in Ritual*

This book, or any other for that matter, is worth little if you are not willing to apply its knowledge to your present situation. Pure and simple, we are all physical beings attached to a material world. If we want to be successful, we must react to our environment in a rational manner, primarily because logic values the system in which it retains momentum. Magick, through the use of imaginary, symbolic tools, and ritual, helps you coordinate your energies with the natural forces and powers of the universe. When you walk in harmony with Mother Nature you can't help but be successful.

"What the mind can imagine, the will can create" should be every aspiring magician's motto. The only thing standing in your way or keeping you from getting what you want is your inability to manifest your thoughts. However, this can be changed through the use of magick and proper ritual procedure.

In the magickal arts and according to *The Donning International Encyclopedic Psychic Dictionary*, a ritual is defined as a "prescribed event or particular ceremony that is built up by tradition, and carries with it a great amount of energy, light, force, and impact."[1] Atmosphere, dress, and symbology contribute to the event, as does the use of repetitious activity. The key factor to effective ritual is repetitious activity. By this I mean doing the exact same thing, in the exact same way, each and every time. This one single point cannot be stressed enough. Spontaneous ritual is fun, but repetitious ritual is effective.

Everything is in a constant state of change and as we are part and party to the universal consciousness we must learn to go with the flow or be swept away by its momentum. If you are going to do magick, you must be willing to accept the unavoidable process of change. It is only when you change your attitude, outlook and way of thinking that things around you begin to change as well.

Change can be very frightening to the poor ego. This is especially true when one begins to dabble in the magickal arts. Once the higher self begins to see the possibilities which lie before it, it will no longer tolerate excuses as to why it doesn't have what it needs and wants. This is something to consider before you get involved. The higher self will tolerate ignorance but not laziness.

The main reason for doing magick is to help you get what you want. This is accomplished through specific ceremonies and rituals designed to distract the ego or conscious self, thus allowing the higher self the time and space it needs to create or bring into being a projected desire. Along with its moment of expression the higher self also needs a certain amount of justification for its actions. There has to be an inner understanding of what is actually

---

[1] Ritual magick is the creation of a specific ceremony, using repetitious activity in a controlled environment, to create or force a change to occur in accordance with your will. The only reason for doing ritual magick is to change something, even if the change is only one of personal attitude.

taking place and why. The higher self accepts logic and facts not fantasy and delusion. When properly presented through ritual, the higher self reacts and produces results.

All magick works when properly executed. It is only a matter of distracting the lower self or ego, long enough for the higher self to be able to get something accomplished. This is done by occupying the childish ego with all sorts of trinkets and things to do. During this time the higher self is able to sneak off and create something of value. This is why tools, symbols and atmosphere are so important. You must totally occupy the lower self, or doubting ego, in order for the higher self to have the freedom and space to produce desirable results.

The easiest and most efficient way to enter into ritual magick is through that which surrounds us. By aligning ourselves with natural forces, becoming aware of cycles and changes in our environment, we begin to flow with the universe. Once caught up in this current of universal movement it is only natural to feel its power. We begin to feel connected too, rather than separated from that which surrounds us.

It is imperative, for magickal purposes, to be able to relate to our surroundings. We must be able to feel the energy flowing through us, combining our individual power with that which already exists. It is only reasonable to take advantage of what is here and now, as this simplifies the entire creation process, and speeds up the time involved in recreating reality.

THE THREE MAJOR REASONS FOR DOING RITUAL

- **Spiritual** The spiritual ritual is usually enacted to align oneself with a specific divine energy source, such as an Archangel, god, and/or goddess.
- **Material** A material ritual, is used to create or manifest a desired goal for the purpose of obtaining something on the material

plane. This could be anything from getting a raise in pay to healing a consenting injured friend.

- **Celebration**   In Wicca, most celebration rituals tend to focus on seasonal Sabbats, the full moon, and personal transitions.

When planning on doing a ritual it is important for your motives or intentions to be clear as they will greatly influence your productivity during ritual. The higher self knows why you are doing something, so be honest with yourself. Your reasons are your own and perfectly justifiable if approached in a sincere manner. The point of doing any ritual is to create a flow of energy, not engage in battle with your higher consciousness.

Once the reason for doing a ritual has been decided upon, and a theme developed, it will be necessary to construct the ceremony itself. When developing any ritual there are four distinct segments which must be dealt with if the ritual is to be effective.

1. The first segment is the **preparation**. This includes altar arrangement, marking the boundary of the ritual space, and casting the magick circle—the psychic energy barrier that separates the ritual area from the surrounding physical realm. Once the circle has been cast the Elemental or Watchtower Guardians are called in and the God and Goddess (if the rite is a spiritual one) are invoked. The invocations draw the special essence of the deity being worked with down into the participant in order to bless and empower the work.

2. The next step in the ritual procedure is that of the **petition**. This describes in some form or another the reason for doing the ritual. It may be a story, a descriptive poem or just a simple prayer to deity. The most important aspect of the petition is the statement it makes regarding the petitioner's desire. During this segment of the ritual, chanting is used to raise energy for the petition to help bring it into reality. This is done by members taking hands and passing energy from one person to the next around the circle. The rhythm and intensity of the chant causes

the energy level to rise within both the individuals and the circle itself. This energy is then directed towards the desired goal.

3. The third segment of the ritual is the **blessing**. This is when symbolic offerings are made, usually for consideration of the ritual petition or for the remembrance of something special that has been received. In addition, the Rite of Union is performed— a ceremony that involves the conjoining of the true masculine and feminine energies of the universe for the purpose of blessing wine and bread.

4. The conclusion of the ritual includes the **dismissing** of the Elemental or Watchtower Guardians and the taking down or closing of the circle. It is during this segment, that the ritual is brought to an end and all of the energies that have been raised are grounded and allowed to dissipate. This segment of the ritual is just as important as the preparation since raised energy needs to be "let go of" in order to be able to work. Another reason for getting rid of the raised energy is that you don't want it to interfere with other projects that may be at cross purpose to each other.

Whenever you write a ritual, it is a good idea to keep the above suggestions in mind. They will help you format your ceremonies in an organized manner so they will be clear in their purpose and in such a way flow smoothly.

To help organize your rituals and magickal works it is good to create a *ritual plan of action*. What this does is express in written form the totality of your intent, as well as what you will need (tools and symbols) to bring it about.

THE RITUAL PLAN OF ACTION

DEFINE YOUR DESIRE AND INTENT

What is it you want? For what reason are you going to do a ritual? Be honest, because your motivation is what will provide the energy and drive to make the ritual Don't be afraid to write down what you want. If you are embarrassed to put your desires into writing because you feel they are dishonorable or without merit then you should not attempt to bring them into manifestation. Besides if you feel the least hesitation in what you are doing, you will not be able to raise the energy needed to bring it about.

CONSTRUCT THE RITUAL

Once you have carefully considered your desire, you will need to write the ritual out just as you plan to perform it. This should be a step by step process and include both liturgy and proper use of symbolism. You will want to align your ritual with the proper planetary forces, time of day, and place or setting where the rite will be performed.

A ritual is like a play and expresses an idea or concept in material form. When properly executed the ritual makes an impression on both the surrounding atmosphere and the consciousness of the individual(s) involved. You might consider this to be a great game of pretend, where you coerce yourself into believing that what you most desire is taking place. In reality you are forcing your intentions on the environment, which creates a space for the desire, enabling it to exist.

PREPARE YOURSELF FOR THE RITUAL

A personal time of meditation and contemplation prior to ritual is essential. You should always take at least a half-hour to an hour to prepare for any ceremony. Just the day-to-day rush and vibrational energies that surrounds us all needs to be balanced out, if we are to function effectively in ritual.

The best way to prepare for any ceremony is with a cleansing bath. This will help get rid of any negativity that you might have been exposed to prior to the ritual. The bath also provides you with time to relax and focus on your desires and the ritual.

An important part of ritual that is often overlooked is "set-up time." This is when you dress, set up the altar and prepare the room or area for the ceremony. Set up time should always be considered part of the ritual itself. Remember, rituals are like plays in which we express a physical desire, in symbolic form, to our higher consciousness. As in any play the props, stage setting, and choreography are an integral part of its effectiveness. Soft, ritualistic (New Age) music, the aroma of incense, and even a small glass of your favorite wine or herbal tea can help set the mood. This is important. You need to be totally relaxed and in the proper frame of mind before you start any ritual.

One thing that helps keep ritual work in perspective, and helps organize spiritual activities is a Ritual Checklist. Generally, the list should begin with the reason for doing the ritual, include set up instructions along with necessary items, and supply the instructions for performing the rite. It serves as your script, directs your actions during the ceremony, and prevents you from making mistakes. I've included a sample checklist, which is on page 50.

Rituals do not necessarily have to be elaborate or complicated to achieve their purpose. In fact, this is where so many make their greatest mistake. They attempt to enlist the power of every conceivable magickal item and incantation known to man. What they end up with is something that resembles an auctioneer at a flea market rather than a practitioner of the magickal arts. On the other hand, a ritual without the appropriate components, energy, and enthusiasm is just as useless.

Ritual should be enjoyable, not something that everyone does because they feel they have to. If you are going to do a ritual, do it correctly. And remember a good ritual, properly constructed and performed always works.

Balance is the key to an effective ritual. It means knowing what, when, and where to use your magickal tools and symbols so they are most effective. You don't see a carpenter carrying every tool he

The Ritual Checklist

Type of Ritual _____

Date of Ritual _____ Moon Phase _____ Place of Ritual _____

Purpose/Intent _____

Necessary Items _____

_____

Special Symbols _____

God and/or Goddess to be Invoked _____

Pre-ritual Meditation _____

_____

Pre-ritual Setup Instructions _____

_____

Special Ritual Instructions _____

_____

RITUAL LITURGY OUTLINE

Preparation and Consecration

   Light Candles _____

   Cast Circle _____

   Call in Guardians _____

   Invoke God and/or Goddess _____

Petition

   Liturgy _____

   Chant _____

   Meditation _____

Blessing

   Ritual Offering _____

   Rite of Union _____

Dismissing

   Dismiss Guardians _____

   Final Blessing of Prayer _____

   Close Down Circle _____

owns to the top of the ladder just to nail in a single board. He surveys the job and takes up only what he needs. Ritual magick is no different. Time should be taken to plan out exactly what you wish to accomplish and the appropriate items collected. Then you take only those tools and symbols needed into the ritual. Use common sense. You only want to distract the lower self, not confuse it to the point of stupefaction.

6

First Steps in Ritual

"The Sole function of a temple is to provide a controlled
environment for magickal work because the temple
is nothing more or less than a workroom,
albeit a special workroom."

—Phillip Cooper, *Basic Magick*

To really understand Wiccan magick one needs to experience it
rather than just intellectualize about it. Magick is something
you learn by doing. And, one of the first things you will want to
learn to do is how to purify and consecrate your working tools.
Purification is the process that removes any negative forces that
may be attached to the object. Consecration then blesses and rein-
forces the object with your feelings and vibrations.

Purification and consecration are an integral part of ritual
magick because they help set the vibratory frequency for the projection of personal power. These special ceremonies help you personalize ritual objects, and attune them to your own physical and
psychic energies. It is this psychic rapport with the tools that turns
them into extensions of your personal magnetism.

The best time to do a ritual of purification and consecration is during the waxing moon.[1] This is the time of new beginnings, when the creative energies are most active. The waxing moon also provides a positive force field to work with. As the consecration of the tools is both positive and the beginning of your magickal work, it is best done during this lunar phase.

The rituals of purification and consecration are simple and do not require a lot of previous experience. All you really need are the objects to be consecrated, a small table to serve as an altar, and the following items:

- A stick of sandalwood incense and an ash catcher
- One white candle
- One bowl of salt, and one filled with water
- A white cloth to cover the altar with

Before you begin the ritual, check to make sure you have everything you need. Place all the required items on the altar. Once everything is in place you will begin by taking your ritual bath. This washes away any negativity you may have picked up during the day, as well as helps relax and prepare you for the rite. For your bath you will need some salt, a white candle, and a stick of your favorite incense.

The Ritual Bath

As the bath water is running, light the white candle saying:

Let the spirit of fire consume all negative thoughts and vibrations.

Place the candle next to the tub and light the incense saying:

Let the essence of air purify my mind and body.

---

[1] The waxing moon is the time between the new and full moon. Almanacs and all Astrological calendars indicate the phases of the moon for each month.

Place the incense next to the tub. Sprinkle some of the salt into the water as you say:

> *Let the elements of earth and water combine to cleanse*
> *and protect me from all negative thoughts and vibrations.*
> *So Mote It Be.*

Relax, and enjoy this quiet time alone. Allow yourself to let go of all the mundane thoughts that have occupied your mind all day. Meditate on what you will be doing in the ritual. When you let the water out of the tub, visualize all of the physical as well as psychic uncleanliness that may have been attached to you going down the drain. You are now clean and ready to proceed with the ceremony.

THE RITUAL OF PURIFICATION

Arrange the following objects on your altar:

Incense (air), to represent your intellectual attributes should be placed on the *Eastern* edge of the table.

Candle (fire), to represent your strength and personal power should be placed on the *Southern* edge of the table.

Bowl of Water (water), to represent your emotions and intuition, is placed on the *Western* edge of the table.

Bowl of Salt (earth), to represent the ability to manifest your desires is placed on the *Northern* edge of the table.

Once this has been done you are ready to begin. Place the tools to be consecrated on top of or under the altar, depending on available space.

Begin by relaxing. Focus your attention as you visualize the immediate area enclosed in a large cone of light; feel the cone surrounding you completely forming a protective barrier between you and the outside world. When you become comfortable with the cone of protection, visualize a shaft of blue-white light (the true spirit of the cosmos) flowing in through the top of the cone, spiraling downward and bathing you in its pure vital energy. This active visualization will force all of the negative energies away from you, and out the bottom of the floor of the cone. When you feel completely safe, protected, and energized, it is time to begin the actual purification of the tools.

Take several deep, relaxing breaths. Pick up the wand and pass it through the incense smoke and candle flame, then sprinkle it with water and salt. *Focus your attention,* see all the negative thoughts and vibrations being drawn out of the tool and dispersed. (You will do the same with each tool.) As you do this say the following:

> *Let now the powers of Air, Fire, Water, and Earth*
> *Cleanse this instrument of intelligence, insight, and wisdom*
> *Of all previous negative thoughts and vibrations.*
> *So Mote It Be.*

Set the wand next to the incense and pick up the athame. Focus your attention on the knife as you pass it through each of the elements. Visualize all negative thoughts leaving as you recite:

> *Let now the powers of Air, Fire, Water, and Earth*
> *Cleanse this instrument of strength, sovereignty, and protection*
> *Of all previous negative thoughts and vibrations.*
> *So Mote It Be.*

Place the athame next to the candle. Pick up the chalice. Focus your attention on the chalice as you pass it through each of the elements. Visualize all negative thoughts leaving as you recite:

> *Let now the powers of Air, Fire, Water, and Earth*
> *Cleanse this instrument of love, expectations, and regeneration*
> *Of all previous negative thoughts and vibrations.*
> *So Mote It Be.*

Position the chalice next to the water. Pick up the pentacle. Focus your attention on the pentacle as you pass it through each of the elements, Again, visualize all negative thoughts leaving as you recite:

Let now the powers of Air, Fire, Water, and Earth
Cleanse this instrument of fortitude, foundation, and form
Of all previous negative thoughts and vibrations.
So Mote It Be.

Place the pentacle next to the salt. Take a few moments to reflect. Look at each tool and see it as a representation of its corresponding element, aligned with that element's power and potential.

THE RITUAL OF CONSECRATION

Now that your tools have been cleansed they are ready for consecration, or to be blessed and dedicated, to your purpose. From this time forward the tools will serve as extensions of your magickal will to help you focus and direct energy. Because of this, they should be filled with your own personal thoughts and vibrations in accordance with the natural elements they each represent.

Beginning with the wand, hold each tool in your strongest hand (right if right-handed and left if left-handed). Feel the alignment the tool has with the element it represents. Allow this feeling to flow through you and into the tool. For example, the wand should feel light, almost weightless. It should be cool to the touch and inspire spiritual feelings and thoughts. The wand fills you with confidence— as you hold it in your hand you know all things are possible.

Pick up the wand and hold it at eye level. Visualize the power and force of the creative spirit in the form of a blue flame flowing into the wand. At the same time fill the wand with your own personal energy and power. It is the force of cosmic energy and your personal power that activates the wand (or any tool) to your magickal will. Repeat this process with each tool in turn as you say:

WAND

I now bless and consecrate thee
To be a wand of enlightenment
That shall ever serve me
In truth, power, and wisdom.

ATHAME

I now bless and consecrate thee
To be as the sword of sovereignty,
That shall ever serve me
In truth, power, and wisdom

CHALICE

I now bless and consecrate thee
To be as the grail of immorality
That shall ever serve me
In truth, power, and wisdom

PENTACLE

I now bless and consecrate thee
To be as a shield of honor
That shall ever serve me
In truth, power, and wisdom

This concludes the purification and consecration ritual. Take a moment to reflect, then "ground and center." This is done by relaxing and letting go of the cone of protection you have created. Inhale and exhale to the count of five. Each time you do this see and feel more of the surrounding cone dissipating, going into the ground, leaving you feeling refreshed and energized.

CREATING SACRED SPACE

Creating sacred space is an essential part of all magickal operations. The actual act itself takes the form of casting or constructing a magick circle. This is done in order to create the proper environment for magickal rites. Once the magick circle has been created it will protect the individuals within its boundary from outside negative influence. The circle or boundary will also help contain the energy raised within its periphery until the time of release.

The first thing you will want to do is to clearly mark out a circle on the floor. The ideal size of a magickal circle is nine feet, but this is ideal not mandatory. In most cases the size will depend on available space and the amount of people taking part in the ritual. Obviously five to seven people will fit nicely into a nine foot circle, fifty will not.

The actual marking of the circle can be done in a variety of ways. If the floor is carpeted, you can mark the circle out with tape or string. Hardwood, cement, or tile can be marked with light colored chalk. If you are working outside then you can mark the earth with your wand or athame. For those who have a special room set aside for their magickal practice the circle may be painted directly onto the floor itself. A large piece of indoor-outdoor carpet cut into a circle serves nicely and can be rolled up and stored when you are finished. Seasonal representations, such as flowers, pine cones or small sprigs of greenery are a welcome touch. The important thing is not so much what you use but the actual physical setting of a boundary line.

Once the circle is marked you will want to identify each of the four Quadrants or elemental directions with symbolic representation. For example, you could use a bell or incense for the East; a sword for the South; a goblet or small cauldron filled with water for the West; and a quartz crystal or a small ornate box filled with earth for the North. Think about what the directions mean to you and use symbols that you can relate to.

When the circle and directions are clearly marked on the floor, place the altar inside of the circle. The position of the altar in the circle is up to the individual, however, most practitioners tend to favor keeping it in the center, facing North. By placing it in the center of the circle it automatically becomes the focal point of the ceremony where all energy and power is directed. Since the altar represents the core of your desire, its central location will only enhance the work at hand.

To create sacred space you begin by standing before the altar. Take several deep, relaxing breaths. When you feel composed and ready, proceed to the Eastern Quadrant with a lighted taper. Pick up the eastern candle, light it as you say the following:

> *I light the East, the home of moonlight and consciousness.*
> *The realm of the spirit.*

Proceed to the South, light the candle as you say:

> *I light the South, the home of fire and inspiration.*
> *The realm of awareness.*

Proceed to the West, light the candle as you say:

> *I light the West, the home of the waves of completeness.*
> *The home of all watery beginnings.*

Proceed to the North, light the candle as you say:

> *I light the North, the home of all that is green and fruitful.*
> *The realm of remembrance.*

The next step is the actual casting of the magick circle. This is accomplished in two parts; first the consecration of the elements (salt and water) and second the projecting of energy onto the marked circle. These combined actions produce the proper atmosphere for a ritual. It is important to understand that as you project the energy onto the physical circle line, you are in reality creating a sphere or total enclosure, rather than just a flat line of energy. When properly completed you will feel as though you are inside a large ball of protective light.

STEP 1. Take your athame or wand, dip the tip into the water saying:

> *Creature of Water cast out from thyself all impurities and uncleanliness of this world.*

STEP 2. Dip your athame or wand into the salt saying:

> *Creature of Earth let only good enter to aid me in my work*

STEP 3. Stir three scoops of salt into the water, see with your mind's eye all the negativity leaving. Now holding your athame or wand in front of you, begin to visualize the energy in the form of a blue flame, coming through into the point of the wand or athame. Begin walking in a deosil (clockwise) manner, pointing your athame or wand down at the edge of the circle as you say:

> *I conjure and create thee O circle of power to be a boundary between the world of men and the realm of the Mighty Ones. A sphere of protection that will preserve and contain all powers raised within. I now consecrate thee to be a place of peace, love, and power. So Mote It Be.*

The final step in creating sacred space is the calling in of the Guardians. To do this you will need to use your athame.[2] Begin in East. Hold the athame at eye level, pointing outward, in the direc-

---

[2]The athame is more suitable for casting the circle and calling in the Guardians because both involve projected energy and imply strength and power—the setting of a field of protection.

tion of the Quadrant. Visualize the Guardian approaching as you say the following:

> *Hear me O Mighty One, Ruler of the Whirlwinds,*
> *Guardian of the Eastern Portal, Watchtower of the East.*
> *I do summon thee forth, to be as witness and shield at this*
> *gateway between the worlds. So Mote It Be.*

Continue to the South. Hold the athame at eye level, pointing outward, in the direction of the Quadrant. Visualize the Guardian approaching as you say the following:

> *Hear me O Mighty One, Ruler of the Solar Orb, Guardian*
> *of the Southern Portal. Watchtower of the South. I do*
> *summon thee forth, to be as witness and shield at this*
> *gateway between the worlds. So Mote It Be.*

Move to the West. Hold the athame at eye level, pointing outward, in the direction of the Quadrant. Visualize the Guardian approaching as you say the following:

> *Hear me O Mighty One, Ruler of the Mysterious Depths,*
> *Guardian of the Western Portal. Watchtower of the West.*
> *I do summon thee forth, to be as witness and shield at this*
> *gateway between the worlds. So Mote It Be.*

Proceed to the West. Hold the athame at eye level, pointing outward, in the direction of the Quadrant. Visualize the Guardian approaching as you say the following:

> *Hear me O Mighty One, Ruler of Forest and Field,*
> *Guardian of the Northern Portal, Watchtower of the*
> *North. I do summon thee forth, to be as witness and shield*
> *at this gateway between the worlds. So Mote It Be.*

Return to the altar. Hold the athame at eye level, and point upward toward the heavens. Visualize an electric-blue field of

energy flowing down and completely covering the sphere of the
encircled area in which you are working with spiritual protection
as you say the following:

> Hear me O Mighty One, Ruler of the Heavenly Vault,
> Guardian of the Divine Kingdom, I do summon forth your
> power and wisdom. For as above, so below, as the universe
> so the soul. As without so within, let now this rite begin.
> So Mote It Be.

At this point, your magickal temple is erected and sacred space
has been created. You may now proceed with your planned spiritual activities. Once inside the circle you will not want to step outside until your ritual activities have been completed, the Guardians
dismissed, and the circle dissolved, banished.

To dismiss the Guardians you will want to retrace your steps,
only moving in the opposite direction. When you created your
sacred space you did so moving in a clockwise or deosil manner,
you will now take down the sacred space moving in a counter-
clockwise or widdershisns direction.

Begin in the North. Hold the athame at eye level, pointing outward, in the direction of the Quadrant, and visualize the Guardian
walking away as you say the following:

> Hear me O Mighty One, Ruler of Forest and Field,
> Guardian of the Northern Portal, Watchtower of the
> North. I thank thee for your blessings and protection.
> Depart unto your earthly realm. I bid thee, Hail and
> Farewell.

Move to the West. Hold the athame at eye level, pointing outward, in the direction of the Quadrant, and visualize the Guardian
walking away as you say the following:

> Hear me O Mighty One, Ruler of the Mysterious Depths,
> Guardian of the Western Portal. Watchtower of the West. I

*thank thee for your blessings and protection. Depart unto
your watery realm. I bid thee, Hail and Farewell.*

Continue on to the South. Hold the athame at eye level, pointing outward, in the direction of the Quadrant, and visualize the
Guardian walking away as you say the following:

*Hear me O Mighty One, Ruler of the Solar Orb, Guardian
of the Southern Portal. Watchtower of the South. I thank
thee for your blessings and protection. Depart unto your
fiery realm. I bid thee, Hail and Farewell.*

Proceed to the East. Hold the athame at eye level, pointing outward, in the direction of the Quadrant, and visualize the Guardian
walking away as you say the following:

*Hear me O Mighty One, Ruler of the Whirlwinds,
Guardian of the Eastern Portal, Watchtower of the East. I
thank thee for your blessings and protection. Depart unto
your airy realm. I bid thee, Hail and Farewell.*

As soon as the Guardians have been dismissed you will want to
extinguish the candles that were placed on the Quadrant compass
points. Again, you will move in a widdershins manner, beginning
with the North as you say the following:

*Let now the North, the home of all that is green and
    fruitful manifest my desires.*

Move to the West, extinguish the candle, and say the following:

*Let now the West, the home of my watery beginnings,
    bring me peace and comfort.*

Continue on to the South, extinguish the candle, and say the
following:

*Let now the South, the home of fire and inspiration, grant
    me strength and power.*

Proceed to the East, extinguish the candle, and say the following:

> *Let now the East, the home of moonlight and*
> *consciousness, endow me with great wisdom.*

Return to the altar, pick up the athame, moving in a widder-shins manner, take up the consecrated circle. Point the athame at the edge of the circle, slowly walk around the boundary of the circle, visualizing the energy of the circle being drawn up and into the athame as you say the following:

> *O circle of power, that has been a boundary of protection*
> *between the world of men and the realm of the mighty*
> *ones, I now dissolve and disband your energy and*
> *protection, and release all powers raised within.*
> *So Mote It Be.*

This completes the process of creating sacred space. If you do not have a special room set aside for your ritual practices, it is a good idea to get into the habit of putting your magickal tools away immediately. By taking care of your ritual tools, you maintain their levels of psychic energy and prevent contamination from outside sources.

As Above, So Below

"If the radiance of a thousand suns were to burst
into the sky, that would perhaps be like the
splendor of the Mighty One."
—Amaury de Riencourt, *The Eye of Shiva*

Since the beginning of time, humankind has looked to the heavens for inspiration. The sun became a God, the moon became a Goddess, and their children, the stars, filled the skies. Majestic mountains, winding rivers, underground caverns, and towering trees became their dwelling places upon the Earth. Their powers were awesome, their conquests are legend, and their love for mankind is unquestionable. They have not died, they have not gone away, they are only waiting for you to bid them welcome—today.

While this book is not about religion, it does stress the presence of higher forces, those of the God and Goddess, within the framework of lunar and seasonal rituals. It is important for us to learn to connect with these forces, or gods, because we have been separated from them for too long. In essence, we need to become friends with the gods in order to share in their knowledge, wisdom, and power.

Within the universe there are certain levels of conscious energy that have always existed. Our ancestors recognized these special forces and gave them individual identity and human characteristics. By doing this, they were able to relate to them on a more intimate and personal level. It was this relationship, with these constructs of conscious energy, that eventually produced the various pantheons of gods and goddesses that now exist.

Initially, it is necessary to understand the nature of these energy forces (or gods) and what they can do for you. The relationship between an individual and his or her god is very much like the relationship between that individual and his or her bank account. However, instead of dealing with a bank and money you are dealing with a god form and energy.

To begin, if you want to have a bank account, you need to choose a bank to put your money in. Then, you open an account by identifying yourself and depositing money into it. At regular intervals you will put more money into the account. For your consideration of support, and use of your money, the bank pays you interest. The more money you put into the bank account, the more interest you receive and the more money you end up with. It is the same thing with the God and Goddess. You find the pantheon of gods you want to work with, then you invest your energy, rather than your money, into them. Obviously, the more time and energy you spend with the god and goddess you have chosen to work with, the stronger the link will become between you, and the more you will benefit from their sovereignty

The first step in choosing a pantheon of gods and goddesses with which to work, is to familiarize yourself with them. This is best done by reading about the gods and learning what types of energy they represent. The next step is to select a major god and goddess from the pantheon who you feel best represents the archetypal masculine and feminine forces of the universe. Once a rapport has been established with these two deities you can proceed to learn about the other members of the pantheon.[1]

The most important thing to remember when choosing a God and Goddess to work with is to choose ones you feel comfortable with. There are a number of ways to do this. You might want to consider your ancestral heritage, geographic associations, or even your personal interests and goals. The only real criteria is to choose your God and Goddess from the same pantheon.

Begin by considering the fundamental energy level of the God and/or Goddess. This is especially important with those deities that come from European pantheons as they represent such divergent lifestyles. For example, a person who is especially refined and artistic and wishes to enhance his or her talents should consider a deity with a similar type of energy. A Greek or Roman deity would be a good choice for this person. However, a Celtic deity would probably be a better choice for a person who is inclined to the robust, earthy, outdoors lifestyle reminiscent of the hills of Ireland. What ever the choice is, it should be based on spiritual awareness and personal feelings for the deity. Remember, only you know how you feel and what will best serve your needs.

The following descriptions of gods and goddesses are from several different pantheons. These are by no means the only ones available to you, and are offered only as suggestions. As you read through these descriptions, allow yourself time to think about each one of them, individually, and ponder what they mean to you.

When you begin reading about the gods, it is a good idea to make notes on how you feel about each one of them. Which ones stir your emotions? Which ones do you instinctively feel affection

[1]Generally the focus of most pantheons is divided into two categories, spiritual and secular. The major deities—the primary God and Goddess—will deal with life issues, spiritual transitions, and morals. The lesser or secondary gods and goddesses usually focus on material objectives (i.e., love, money, fertility, and success).

toward? Which ones represent the concepts you are most interested in working with? Above all, which ones do you want to give your energy to, and become friends with? If you take the time to consider each of the gods individually, it will make your final selection process much easier.

Selecting a god and/or goddess to work with can be approached in various ways. You can look to your ancestral heritage for insight into your cultural conditioning. You might want to use personal interests or previous religious training to help you decide. Some people find it helpful to study ancient myths and legends, as these seem to inspire and encourage the searching soul.

The most important thing to remember when choosing a god and goddess is to *choose the ones you feel comfortable with.* Just because your closest friend is working with Isis doesn't necessarily mean you should work with her as well. If you feel more comfortable with Cerridwen, work with her. No matter who you choose, the choice is yours and should be based on your feelings. Only you know how you feel and what will best serve your needs.

When reading through the list of gods and goddesses you will notice each has been assigned specific, symbolic, correspondences. These correspondences serve as communication links between you, and your chosen god form. When you incorporate one or more of these symbolic correspondences into a magickal rite, you are in essence extending an invitation to that deity—to join with you. By combining your energy with that of the gods, you intensify the ritual experience and magnify your personal power.

The following suggestions will help you learn to work with the god and goddess of your choice.

- Buy or make a statue of the deity and place it on your altar. Once a day, go before the statue and speak to it, just as you would to a close friend.
- Burn candles in the corresponding colors to the deity statue when you are meditating.
- Make a robe of the primary color, which corresponds to your deity. Wear this during your meditations and rituals.

- Make a necklace out of the suggested stones to wear during your ceremonies.
- Use the corresponding plants in your incenses and oils you prepare for use during ritual.
- Place the deity's sacred objects on your altar during ritual.
- Incorporate their symbolic animals into your ceremonies or place pictures of them near your ritual area.
- Combine all of the above suggestions and make a shrine to your deity so the energy is available when you wish to work with it.

Selected Pantheons—The Goddess and the God

Celtic

The Goddess dominates much of the Celtic culture. Although there are many male deities, they usually take second place to female deities, who represent the land and the life-giving, as well as destroying, aspects of nature.

Cerridwen   The Celtic mother goddess of the moon and grain. She is especially known for her fearsome death totem, a white corpse-eating sow. Cerridwen is associated with Astarte or Demeter and her harvest celebrations express her ability to both give life and take it away.

Cerridwen is also known as the goddess of inspiration and knowledge because of her inexahustable cauldron[2] in which she brewed a magick draught called "greal." This draught would give inspiration and knowledge to any who drank of it.

Cerridwen's concepts are expressed clearly in the myth about Gwion Bach. According to the story, a young boy named Gwion Bach got some of the liquid from the cauldron on his finger, and the liquid gave him knowledge. Since the liquid was meant for someone else, Cerridwen relentlessly pursued him in many disguises. Finally, when she caught up to him, he turned into a grain

---

[2]This cauldron was called Amen. The cauldron is considered to be the symbol of life and death and regeneration. It is symbolic of the womb and its creation process.

Correspondences for Cerridwen

Summon Cerridwen for inspiration, knowledge, and wisdom.

Archetype	Crone, initiator
Expression	Mother of inspiration
Time	Full moon, midnight
Season	Harvest (winter)
Object	Cauldron, cup
Number	Three (combinations of three)
Color	Green, blue green, silver or white
Animal	Sow, hen, greyhound, otter, hawk
Tree	Elder, Yew
Plant	Corn, barley, hellebore, patchoully, mimosa, belladonna
Stone	Moonstone, beryl, chalcedony

of wheat and she a hen. She swallowed the grain, giving birth to a male child nine months later. Immediately, Cerridwen set the baby adrift upon the river. He was later discovered and in time became the great bard, Taliesin.

Cernunnos   The Celtic god of vegetation, fertility, and the Underworld, Cernunnos is the stag god, Lord of the Beasts, and master of woodland animals. His name means "Horned One" and he is usually depicted with ram's horns and serpents. His horns are a symbol of strength, power, and virility and the snakes are phallic and symbolic of regeneration.

Cernunnos can be seen as part man and part beast. He is the one who guards the portals of the Underworld and ushers those seeking transformation into the mysteries. He is the giver of life and the bringer of death. Like most horned gods, he is concerned with the Earth and how human life parallels its rhythms and cycles. Of prime

---

Correspondences for Cernunnos

Summon Cernunnos for strength, transition, and virility.

Archetype	Guardian, regenerator
Expression	Father of life
Season	Summer
Time	Noon day sun
Object	Torc necklace, horns, cornucopia, stang
Number	Six
Color	Red, orange, yellow, sometimes black or brown
Animal	Stag, ram, serpent, dog, eagle
Tree	Oak
Plant	Benzoin, bay, mistletoe, orange, juniper, sun flower, marigold
Stone	Agate, jasper, carnelian

---

importance is the idea of growing and becoming strong to ensure the survival of life, the land, and all that resides upon it.

GREEK

Demeter The goddess of vegetation, fertility, and the fruitful Earth. Grain crops were favored by her, especially those of barley and corn. She was the foundress of agriculture and the civic rite of marriage. Her mysteries, which were called the "Thesmophoria" were held each April.

Demeter had several consorts, including Zeus and Poseidon. It was Zeus in the form of a bull, who tricked her, making her mother of Persephone. Hades, Demeter's brother, abducted Persephone and took her to the underworld where he made her his wife. Demeter roamed the Earth weeping in search of Persephone. During this time the entire world remained barren. Zeus took pity

Correspondences for Demeter

Summon Demeter for love, fertility, magick, and prosperity.

Archetype	Mother, fertility
Expression	Patroness of the mysteries
Time	Full moon
Season	Spring, summer
Object	Torch, scepter, water jar, corn dolly
Number	Three, thirteen
Color	Cornflower blue, yellow, silver
Animal	Horse, dolphin, dove
Tree	Hawthorne
Plant	Corn, barley, bean, sunflower, pennyroyal, poppy, rose, wheat
Stone	Turquoise, peridot, pearl, sapphire, moonstone

upon the Earth and Demeter. He made an agreement with Hades that Persephone spend part of the year in the Underworld with her husband Hades and the rest of the year upon the Earth with Demeter. This return to the Earth brought back spring and all life once again blossomed forth.

Zeus The supreme deity in Greek mythology. He was the son of Kronos and Rhea, and was considered to be the "wise council." As a composite figure, the sky god of the Greeks was active in the daily concerns of the world. Because of his involvement with man's affairs, he was venerated as a ruling father figure rather than as a creator deity.

Zeus governed the sky and all atmospheric phenomena. He had dominion over the winds, clouds, rain, and the destructive thunder and lightening. He was depicted as a robust and mature man, with

---

Correspondences for Zeus

Summon Zeus for wisdom, legal matters, business partnerships, success, and strength.

Archetype	Father, ruler/king
Expression	Ruler of the sky, king of the gods
Time	Noon to midnight
Season	Summer, fall, and winter
Object	Thunder bolt, scepter, crown, dagger
Number	One
Color	Royal purple, dark blue, gold
Animal	Eagle, goat, cuckoo, elephant
Tree	Oak, poplar, alder
Plant	Olive, ambergris, violets, apple, mistletoe, mastic, fenugreek, mint
Stone	Diamond, amethyst, chalcedony

---

wavy or curly hair that matched his thick beard. Zeus often wore a crown of oak leaves, carried a thunderbolt, and had an eagle at his feet.

Like most of the Olympian gods, Zeus had many lovers and beget many children. Some of his unions included Metis (wisdom), who knew more things than all the gods and men together. Themis, the daughter of Uranus and Gaia, was another of his loves. She represented the law that regulates both physical and moral order. He finally married Hera and she became the first lady of Olympus.

EGYPTIAN

Isis (Greek for Aset) The Egyptian goddess whose name means throne. Isis is the personification of the great Goddess in

Correspondences for Isis

Summon Isis for love, marriage, and protection.

Archetype	Mother, protectress
Expression	Mistress of magick
Time	New moon
Season	Spring or summer
Object	Thet (knot or buckle), scepter, cup, horns, mirror
Number	Two or eight
Color	Sky blue, green, gold, white
Animal	Snake, goose, owl, hawk, ram
Tree	Fig, willow
Plant	Lotus, lily, narcissus, myrtle, myrrh, iris, date
Stone	Lapis, aquamarine, sapphire

her aspect of maternal devotion. She is the daughter of Seb and Nut, wife and sister of Osiris, and mother to Horus. She is always represented as a woman and wears on her head a miniature throne, which is also the hieroglyph for her name. Her headdress is also sometimes depicted as a solar disk with horns.

Myth and legend confirm Isis as the true wife and mother. When her husband, Osiris, was killed by his jealous brother, Set, she spared no pains in finding his hidden body. Once she found it, Set recaptured it and cut it into fourteen pieces. He then scattered these pieces throughout the land. Isis, hunted all the pieces down and magickally reconstituted the body. She then made love with Osiris, conceived, and gave birth to Horus.

Isis was worshiped as "the great magick" who protected her son Horus from predators and other dangers. Because of this, it was believed she protected mortal children from the perils of daily life.

Correspondences for Osiris

Summon Osiris for court cases, criminal matters, and creative endeavors.

Archetype	King, priest
Expression	Father of stability and growth
Time	Setting sun
Season	Fall, winter
Object	Djed, crook, flail, menat, was (scepter)
Number	Seven, fourteen, twenty-eight
Color	Gold, yellow, green, white
Animal	Hawk, Jackle, ape, bull
Tree	Cypress, thorn
Plant	Acacia, ivy, papyrus, orris, lily, storax, bay, Frankincense, dittany
Stone	Topaz, quartz crystal, carnelian

Osiris   The symbol the Divine in mortal form. He is the personification of physical creation and its cycles of birth, life, death, and return. He is the highest of all powers, the King who brought civilization to the land of Egypt. He is husband and brother to Isis, father of Horus, and son of Seb and Nut.

Osiris was treacherously murdered by his brother, Set, who was considered to be the power of evil and darkness. After his death and resurrection, Osiris became the lord of the Underworld and the judge of the dead. He presides in scenes of judgment, when the heart of the deceased is weighed against the feather of Ma-at and Thoth records the verdict.

Osiris is usually portrayed as a mummified, bearded man wearing the white crown of the North. Around his neck is an elaborate pectoral necklace and the menat counterpoise (a symbolic piece of jewelry that consisted of a broad necklace with several rows of

beads gathered into a long counterweight). He carries the shep-
herd's crook, the symbol of sovereignty and responsibility, and the
flail that separates the wheat from the chaff.

Assyro-Babylonian

Ishtar In Babylonian scripture, Ishtar was called the "Light of
the World, Leader of Hosts, and Opener of the Womb." She was
also the "Lady of Battles" and considered to be valiant among the
goddesses. She was the "goddess of the morn and goddess of the
evening" and the Divine personification of the planet Venus.

Fertility and all aspects of creation were Ishtar's epiphany.
Sacred prostitution was an integral part of her cult, and was looked
upon with respect. Prostitution, like a lot of other things, over the
span of time has been misinterpreted. The original meaning of the
word *prostitute* was "to stand on behalf of" and was considered to
be sacred work for a woman. It was through sexual intercourse

---

Correspondences for Ishtar

Summon Ishtar for love, pleasure, and Divine guidance.

Archetype	Virgin, queen
Expression	Divine harlot, patroness of pleasure
Time	Full moon
Season	Spring
Object	Bow and quiver, sickle of the moon, star,
Number	Seven
Color	Green, blue-green, sapphire blue
Animal	Lion, fish
Tree	Apple, cherry
Plant	Yarrow, woodruff, violet, orchid, rose, foxglove
Stone	Rose quartz, pink tourmaline, emerald, azurite

with the priestesses of Ishtar's temple that men were allowed to experience the state of bliss associated with the Divine union. Prior to Christianity, sex and giving birth were considered channels through which the Divine energy of the gods poured. To be a temple prostitute was to validate and strengthen, or stand on behalf of, the highest potentials of the Goddess herself—those of sacred union and making.

Even today, Ishtar's image can be found in many works of art, including Assyrian cylinder seals, vases, and friezes. She is very easy to recognize because of her symbols, which always appear with her: the eight-pointed star, the crescent moon, and the vessel containing the waters of life.

Tammuz   The mortal king in whom the god or spirit of fertility was incarnate and who dies a violent death. He was an agricultural divinity and vegetation spirit who manifested in the seed of corn.

Correspondences for Tammuz

Summon Tammuz for fertility, business success, and agricultural matters.

Archetype	Divine victim
Expression	King, god of the land
Time	Setting sun
Season	Fall, winter
Object	Cross, scythe, sheaf, flute
Number	Two
Color	Gold, orange, brown, green
Animal	Lyon, phoenix, fish
Tree	Elder, yew, ivy
Plant	Bay, laurel, corn, frankincense, barley, fumitory, juniper
Stone	Jasper

The myth of Tammuz recounts the cycle of life and death. The god is killed by an enemy and his death brings about the stagnation of all natural life. The goddess, Ishtar, bewailed him and set out to retrieve him. He was found and liberated with the help of his son. With his resurrection, nature and especially all vegetation, revived.

NORSE

Freya The highly and most revered Teutonic goddess whose name means "Lady." She was known as the Fair One and was famous for her great beauty. Freya was primarily the goddess of love, but oversaw war, life, and death as well. She is patroness to housewives, mothers, and women of great strength and power. In times of battle, Freya selected the most noble of the fallen warriors, whom she then personally carried to the realm of the gods.

Correspondences for Freya

Summon Freya for love, all things that concern the hearth and home, strength and power.

Archetype	Virgin, lover
Expression	Priestess of love, life, and death
Time	New to full moon
Season	Spring, summer
Object	Brisingamen, feather cloak, wings
Number	Five
Color	Silver, pink, pale blue or green
Animal	Cat, hawk, boar
Tree	Apple, holly
Plant	Cowslip, crocus, rose, lilac, primrose, sweet pea
Stone	Blue or pink tourmaline, emerald, chrysocolla

Freya appeared to her worshipers in a falcon-plumed cloak under which she wore a magickal necklace called Brisingamen, whose power could not be resisted. She would ride through the moon-lit sky in a chariot drawn by cats or sometimes a huge golden boar.

In Norse mythology, Freya was wife and priestess to Odin and though she loved him, was often unfaithful. When Odin left her, she wept tears of gold. Assuming various names, she searched for him through all of the nine Nordic worlds. She slept with dwarves, was delivered into the hands of giants, and then finally rescued and returned to the Earth.

Odin   Often called Woden or Wotan, was the primary diety, or the All Father "God" of Valhalla, the Norse pantheon. He was revered for his great wisdom and ability in battle. He was considered to be both father and victorious warrior. Because of his

Correspondences for Odin

Summon Odin for increase in knowledge, wisdom, strength, and power.

Archetype	Warrior, father
Expression	Priest, Shaman
Time	Sunrise
Season	Winter
Object	Sword, shield, runes, robe
Number	One
Color	Gold, red
Animal	Wolf, raven, horse
Tree	Birch, oak
Plant	Holly, mistletoe, juniper, gum arabic, marigold, angelica, mastic
Stone	Diamond, bloodstone, garnet

authority, he was consulted by all the other gods and men alike. Odin was wise in the ways of the world and possessed immense powers.

The myths of Odin describe him as always being involved with the people, taking an interest in their daily lives and helping out in family matters. Often he would roam the world alone accompanied only by a pair of ravens and a pair of wolves. It is said that he rode upon an eight-legged steed named Slepnir, which represented time itself and was followed by Odin's son, who personified the yearly reborn spirit of life.

What sets Odin apart from the other gods is his quest for knowledge. He treasured it so highly that he gave his right eye for it. At one point he tied himself to a tree and remained there for nine days and nine nights in order to gain wisdom from it. He is the ultimate priest for God, and an example to all men because of his ability to gain knowledge.

8

Magick, Ritual, and the Tarot

> "The idea of psychic power and psychic prediction
> is no longer the sole pastime of the superstitious; instead
> it is a reality that needs to be taken more seriously,
> a fact of life that should be examined more sensibly."
> —David Lemieuz, *Forbidden Images, The Secrets of the Tarot*

It is a common practice to consult the Tarot or some other form of divination before engaging in a magickal operation. Through divination, we are able to determine the "true" or "original" motives behind our actions—these thoughts and ideas that might be blurred or blown out of proportion during emotional distress. Since we all overreact in the heat of anger or passion, by taking the time to examine our motives, and those circumstances that surround the work, we are able to avoid possible pitfalls and mistakes.

The Tarot, like most divination systems, allows us to tap into the collective unconscious. It is this subconscious awareness within all humans as a group, that psychiatrist Carl Jung (1875–1961) believed was organized in symbols. These symbols represent archetypal concepts that speak to the unconscious and reveal hidden truths and knowledge of the past, present, and future.

We all suffer moments of doubt and wonder if what we are doing is correct. Many times this self-doubt keeps us from doing what we should and what will enhance our lives. By having a system of divination that checks and balances our motivations (which are what drive or initiate actions) we can eliminate many of the fears we face and begin doing instead of just wishing.

THE TAROT

The Tarot is a deck of highly symbolic cards that is used to look into the past, confirm the present, and foresee the future. The deck consists of seventy-eight cards—twenty-two Major Arcana and the fifty-six Minor Arcana. The Major Arcana has symbolic pictures on them, and represents significant phases an individual confronts in life, while the Minor Arcana resembles the cards in a regulation playing deck and contains suites and numbers.

THE MAJOR ARCANA

As the primary source of information, the Major Arcana is divided into three sections referred to as the Septenary. Each Major Arcana card bears a title, a Roman style number from 0—the Fool, to XXI—the World, and represent a station in life (or gate) through which the 0—Fool must pass. As the only unnumbered card in the deck, the Fool represents the state of nothingness or lack of form from which all things begin—the dynamic energy and motion that causes one to act on impulse or take the first step.

The first septenary of the Major Arcana includes: I—the Magician, II—the High Priestess, III—the Empress, IV—the Emperor, V—the Hierophant; VI—the Lovers, and VII—the Chariot. This group represents the beginning of the Fool's journey. As a youth, the Fool must discover the joys and sorrows of dealing with authority, teachers, emotions, and choices.

The second septenary includes VIII—Strength, IX—the Hermit, X—the Wheel of Fortune, XI—Justice, XII—the Hanged Man, XIII—Death, and XIV—Temperance. Now an adult, the Fool must begin to address his/her own strengths and weaknesses, ego, place within the cosmos, spiritual issues, and the ability to maintain control.

The third septenary concludes with XV—the Devil, XVI—the Tower, XVII—the Star, XVIII—the Moon, XIX—the Sun, XX—Judgment, XXI—the World. This is the final leg of the Fool's journey. He or she must now learn to accept responsibility for the past, and have enough insight to see into the future. Soon the mysteries and joys of the universe will be revealed, and the Fool will reap the rewards or consequences of his/her actions.

Philosophically, the Fool stands alone in the deck, without a number and therefore without identity. The Fool represents pure potential—the clay from which the individual's personality is molded

The Minor Arcana

The Minor Arcana is divided into four suits Swords, Wands, Cups, and Pentacles. Each of these suites represents one of the four basic elements and corresponding human attribute, Air—thinking, Fire—acting, Water—feeling, and Earth—sustaining.

Each suite of the Minor Arcana begins with an an ace that represents a time of beginning and a season. The Ace of Wands is associated with the Spring, the Ace of Swords, summer, the Ace of Cups, fall, and the Ace of Pentacles, winter. In addition there are four court cards: the Page representing youth, the Knight representing adulthood, the Queen representing feminine maturity, and the King representing masculine maturity.

In addition to the symbolism expressed by each card, the reader must also consider the position in which the card rests. Once the deck has been shuffled, not all of the cards will face the same direction. When they are laid out in a pattern for reading, some of the cards will be right-side up, and some will be reversed. If the card is reversed, then its power and potential are diminished, and this must be taken into consideration. This does not imply an opposite meaning, just a decrease in capacity.

THE DIVINATORY MEANING OF THE CARDS

THE MAJOR ARCANA

0 The Fool
The Fool represents the absence of all things real or imagined. This is the place from where we begin—the time and space before decision or choice is made. *Reversed*: Lack of effort, an irresponsible person or fear. About to make an unwise choice.

I The Magician (Mercury)
Will and determination to see an idea through, skill, talent, ability, and choice. Strong will and ability to utilize one's innate faculties. *Reversed*: Abuse of power, lack of concentration, and trickery.

II The High Priestess (Moon)
Knowledge, education, wisdom, creative ability, feminine influence, perception, and self-motivation. Mystery and spiritual matters revealed. *Reversed*: Egotism, nothing hidden at this time, vanity, and superficiality.

III The Empress (Venus)
The Earth Mother. The ability to create; good harvest, a time of plenty, and material gain. *Reversed*: Poor health, wasteful, and unstable

IV The Emperor (Aries)
The King. Someone able to be a leader—leadership qualities; in a position of authority, and in control of their life. *Reversed*: Overbearing, out of control, and wrong use of authority.

V The Hierophant (Taurus)
The High Priest. Religious influence, conformity, someone who is inspirational—the gateway to higher consciousness. *Reversed*: A bit unconventional, a nonconformer.

VI The Lovers (Gemini)

True love and equality between a man and a woman, the choice between sacred and profane love, the situation calls for a choice—a decision. *Reversed*: Negative effect on love or love affair, possibility of separation or divorce. Be careful of your choice.

VII The Chariot (Cancer)

Triumph, success. Someone in control over the elements of nature, the warrior who has conquered on all planes. *Reversed*: Lack of control, too many decadent desires, an unethical victory.

VIII Strength (Leo)

Spiritual power, the ability to overcome material desire, balance between the spiritual and carnal nature. A well-balanced body and mind. *Reversed*: Letting aspects of the lower self take control.

IX The Hermit (Virgo)

The teacher. A time for soul searching; someone looking for a teacher, and the teacher is provided when the time is right. *Reversed*: Very closed mind, stubborn, refusal to take help or listen; lack of personal growth.

X Wheel of Fortune (Jupiter)

Fate, chance, and destiny; cause and effect; karma, change of luck. The ability to change the future if right moves are made at this time. *Reversed*: Failure of an enterprise, setbacks, need courage to go on with projects.

XI Justice (Libra)

A fair and just outcome; good instinct and perception; putting things in order, finally being able to achieve balance. *Reversed*: An unfair judgement; poor choices and decisions.

XII The Hanged Man

Spiritual awareness, the happiness and assuredness that spiritual awareness brings; the reversal of one's current lifestyle and ways;

letting go of the material. *Reversed*: Selfish and materialistic; concerned only with physical and material.

XIII   Death (Scorpio)

The end of a particular phase of life; a major change is due; this is not physical death, just the ending of something; all things come to an end sooner or later; renewal; change as the old is outworn and of no use. *Reversed*: Catastrophe, disorder, and panic.

XIV   Temperance (Sagittarius)

Moderation and control in all actions and affairs, someone capable of diplomacy, even temperament and harmonizing. *Reversed*: Unstable efforts and actions; too many mood swings and emotional instability.

XV   The Devil (Capricorn)

Wrong use of force; in bondage to the material world; involved in negative or black magick; greed, lust, and perversion. *Reversed*: Rejection of the material, a turn to higher forces for help, bondage to material world is broken.

XVI   The Tower (Mars)

Sudden change; sudden inspiration, and realization; a traumatic change that will bring about positive growth—the forces of karma at work. *Reversed*: Future lacks insight and ability to let go, time to rebuild.

XVII   The Star (Aquarius)

Insight, inspiration, and understanding; someone with unique and different ideas, the humanitarian who wants to improve the world; a new life and an openness to new ideas and concepts. *Reversed*: Doubt and pessimism. Failure to find happiness.

XVIII   The Moon (Pisces)

Psychic powers, a mystical individual, one with hidden talents. Time for feelings to come out—look carefully at a situation that can be illusionary. *Reversed*: Storms to be waited out, what was unclear now becomes clear. A mystery is solved.

XIX   The Sun (Sun)
Happiness, pleasure, and joy; the ability to understand; a very positive time with lots of energy and warmth; a time of love, joy, success, and attainment. *Reversed*: Loss and unhappiness, failure in matters of importance.

XX   Judgment (Pluto)
Personal consciousness blends into universal consciousness, release and liberation, final attainment and fulfillment. *Reversed*: Weakness, disillusion, fear of death, failure to find happiness.

XXI   The World (Saturn)
Triumph in all undertakings, deserved rewards realized, peace and joy in the home, success, reaping the rewards of a life well lived, completion. *Reversed:* Success yet has to be won, fear of change, earthbound. Strong attraction to the material.

MINOR ARCANA

WANDS

Ace   New beginnings; enterprise, new things starting, possible birth in family, new job, career, new way of life. *Reversed*: Lack of effort, not trying hard enough. Take a second look.

Two   Sign of achievement; future looks good, persevere, have courage; may mean business partnership. *Reversed*: Foundations laid may not bring desired results. Have patience. Reorganize.

Three   Someone willing to help; partnership, business venture may prosper. *Reversed*: Talents and skills being wasted. Direction is needed.

Four   Harmony peace and satisfaction, may be beginning of romance, enjoy results of work. *Reversed*: Positive improvement, well on way to achievement. If you care, show it. Be thankful for what you have.

Five   Opposing energy, struggle, you are feeling stress, situation calls for clarity. *Reversed*: Harmony and sense of peace will prevail. Don't be defensive.

Six   Have faith, you can win; you are going to succeed; relationships will get better. *Reversed:* Unable to get it together, be careful not to let pride get in the way.

Seven   You are well blessed with inner strength; strong character; work well under pressure. *Reversed:* Look for strength from within. Don't be indecisive. He who hesitates is lost.

Eight   Acceleration in your affairs, movement, fast advancement, news coming, travel. *Reversed:* Apprehension creates an insecure feeling. Learn to control emotions.

Nine   Able to maintain control of interests, hold onto what you have, you have the strength to see things through. *Reversed:* Not applying yourself, lack of initiative. You are not properly prepared.

Ten   You have been under pressure, indicates an oppressive burden, darkness before dawn. *Reversed*: Talent, ability, and skills used in the wrong way. Clever person trying to unload burdens onto others.

Page   Indication of message from a near friend; a young person, boy or girl (fair hair, blue eyes). *Reversed*: Uncomfortable relationship with a person who is domineering.

Knight Young man will cause change, expect someone to present thoughts that will be advantageous to business (fair hair, blue eyes). *Reversed:* Lack of energy, frustration, and indecision; look out for jealousy.

Queen Woman who has attractive personality, sensible and mature, can be most helpful; gives good advice. *Reversed*: Someone that is narrow-minded. Often takes a domineering approach.

King A man secure in business, strong, and generous (fair hair and blue eyes); excellent leadership qualities. *Reversed:* Indication of a disagreement or dispute, you may feel uneasy with his lack of tolerance.

CUPS

Ace Beginnings of love, joy, health; new spiritual insight; making a new start. *Reversed*: Egotistical and self-centered. Need for balance.

Two Deep friendship or love between a man and a woman, a beautiful start to a new romance. *Reversed*: Loss of balance in a close relationship. Pride destroys love.

Three Happy conclusion, success, and beginning of a new lifestyle. Something good is on the way. Indication of metaphysical interests. *Reversed*: Overindulgence, circumstances have changed; what was good now causes pain.

Four Discontent and bored, couldn't care less what happens, too much of a good thing, life is too easy, won't even make an effort. *Reversed*: New relationship now possible, great desire to accomplish something.

Five You find it difficult to explain the turmoil you feel inside, marriage or relationship appears to be breaking up. *Reversed*: Things now looking better, there is hope, could be happy news.

Six   From the past will come happiness, possible to meet an old friend, possible to make a new friend who you will have a lot in common with. *Reversed*: Living in the past, rewards may be delayed, something you are looking forward to will be postponed.

Seven   You may be experiencing difficulties in making a decision; be realistic, narrow down your choices. *Reversed*: On the right track, you should pursue your goal; don't give up your ideas.

Eight   There is a need to search for a deeper meaning in life, you have a need for spiritual fulfillment, dissatisfaction with the way things are. *Reversed*: Interests lie in material pleasures, you desire a complete change, could mean new love is on the way.

Nine   This is the wish card. With this card in the spread your wishes will come true, much happiness is assured and material gain. *Reversed*: Wish will not be fulfilled, insufficient fund for a project, a feeling of being deprived.

Ten   Indication of marriage, things looking bright, possible trips that will bring good fortune. *Reversed:* Depression, things not looking good at this time.

Page   Young person (light brown hair, hazel eyes); can mean news of a birth or wonderful plan, idea, or program. *Reversed*: You will be offered help by a young person; lethargic, not much desire to plan ahead.

Knight   Someone you may know may have opposing views. A young man can offer interesting inventions or proposals.

Reversed: Look before you leap. Half-truths promote difficulties.

Queen   Sensitive lady who relies on her intuitive ability rather than common sense; lady with perception, can see ahead. *Reversed*: Lacks depth, unwise to relate secrets to, means well but is not reliable.

King   A reliable and respected man, quiet type of a man who keeps his emotions hidden; could be a church leader or teacher. *Reversed*: Avoid entanglement with this man, he is not what he seems to be; double-dealing.

SWORDS

Ace   Beginnings, the seeds of success are now taking root, anxiously expecting the worst to happen, forget the past and put your energies into new projects. *Reversed*: Look for weak spots in your plans, make sure all is in order, goals not realized at this time.

Two   You don't know what to do, emotions are involved; difficult to decide; need for insight. *Reversed*: Things now happening, you are now able to make decisions, affairs moving fast.

Three   Loss and sorrow; it is hard to bear the pain, separation, or loneliness; upheaval in family, misfortune, loved ones separate. *Reversed*: Same as above but less tension—circumstances not so severe.

Four   Feeling of being cut off; a time to step back, period of rest; the shadow over you is slowly passing away. *Reversed*: Back into action again, good opportunities ahead.

Five   Lack of sensitivity, interested only in self-gain; ruling by force; a chance to lose by theft. *Reversed:* If there is no change in attitude, loss will occur.

Six   Difficult cycle now ending, possible long journey.
             Reversed: Feeling of being locked into a difficult
             situation, look deep within for answer.

Seven   Things may not work out the way you have planned,
             one thing after another, sheer bad luck. *Reversed:* Listen
             carefully, someone may offer advice that will help;
             don't let false pride get in your way.

Eight   Unable to make a decision; have experienced hurt or
             anxiety; vision blocked, feeling of being trapped.
             Reversed: Pressure is now beginning to be released, Soon
             there will be relaxation from fears.

Nine   Despair and anxiety are causing misery and sense of
             hopelessness; could indicate serious illness or tragedy.
             Reversed: Tomorrow holds promise and hope; looks like
             good news is coming.

Ten   Extreme unhappiness, depression, and deep sorrow;
             sense of loss, can mean separation, *Reversed:* Cycle of
             events now changing, coming out of bad times.

Page   A young person's activities could be causing you
             concern (brown hair or black hair/eyes), someone on
             the defensive. *Reversed:* Someone who is unpredictable,
             look further into situation.

Knight   Young man has good intentions, bold, overbearing.
             Reversed: Someone is opposed to your plans, steer clear
             of this person.

Queen   Lady with a sharp wit, a serious and good counselor,
             spiritual depth by prolonged study. *Reversed:* Intolerant,
             narrow-minded, finds fault with everyone, unwise to
             confide in her.

King   A man of authority, associated with law; he is most reliable, take his advice. *Reversed*: Inclined to be strict to the point of cruelty, he does not appear to have any compassion, stern.

PENTACLES

Ace   Beginning of prosperity, everything is great; good foundations bring good results. *Reversed*: False security, great plans may not materialize, overly possessive regarding money.

Two   Trying to cope with two situations at the same time, someone who is able to cope. Much would get done if a decision was made. *Reversed*: Doubtful plans will run smoothly, need to think of a new way, keep on trying.

Three   Well-informed, great skill, ability, and talent; efforts will be rewarded. *Reversed*: Insufficient experience, you need to learn more.

Four   Strongly attached to the material; greedy, likes power; will work very hard to attain wealth. *Reversed*: Confronted with loss or obstacles, need to establish new plans.

Five   Take time to review what is happening in your life, loss and sorrow, don't give up even if you feel it is best. *Reversed*: Accept karmic lesson, try to understand what has happened, accept lesson, try to look ahead.

Six   Happy atmosphere, about to enjoy the fruits of your labor; you receive what you have earned; good things happening, could be promotion. *Reversed*: Unsatisfactory situation, not satisfied; unsettled feelings.

Seven   A change in cycle that will affect your income; growth through good, hard work and effort. *Reversed:* Anxiety, depression; possibly related to finances.

Eight   Strong; established; prepared for the future; not receiving much money but learning and on the right track. *Reversed:* Going about things in the wrong way, too concerned about the ego.

Nine   A feeling of being complete, but for some reason still seeking; realize the material is not all there is in life. *Reversed:* Time to look over goals, meditation on what you should be doing is necessary at this time.

Ten   Beginning to feel secure, finances beginning to look better, attainment and recognition. *Reversed:* One problem after another, nothing seems to be going the way you want it to, money problems.

Page   A young person who enjoys studying, white or dark hair, a person will be giving you good news. *Reversed:* Someone who is moody and goal-oriented, love of the material.

Knight   A young man who will take his time and see that the job is well done; needs constant motivation, good with money. *Reversed:* Irresponsible, impatient, money and hard work not important to this young man.

Queen   A creative lady with many talents, will be good in business. *Reversed:* Too much dependence on others, inclined to be lazy; will often neglect responsibilities.

King   This man is good with money matters, good job or
position in industry, he is generous and friendly.
Reversed: Very materialistic, easy to bribe, skims the
surface of everything, does not use talents wisely.

A SAMPLE TAROT CARD LAYOUT

The following spread, called a European spread, is used to obtain
a yes or no answer to a question, and then provide insight regarding the answer. Shuffle the cards, and then spread them face down
in front of you. As you ask your question, run your hand over the
top of the cards. Pull seven cards from the pack and lay them face
down in a single row. Turn each card over individually. If the
majority of the cards are right side up the answer is YES, if the
majority are reversed, the answer is NO. To determine the reason
for the answer, begin with the left two cards, which represent the
past events. It is these events that have lead to the present three
middle cards. These three cards represent the present forces surrounding you and the course of action you should take. Your present actions are what will determine your future outcome,
represented by the two remaining cards on the right.

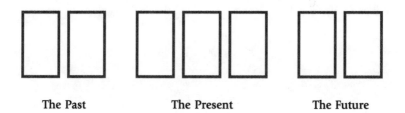

The Past   The Present   The Future

This spread is extremely valuable if you are trying to determine if your course of action is reasonable. For example, you could ask "Is this a good time to approach my boss for a pay raise?" If the answer is Yes, then it might be advisable to do a simple spell to increase your self-confidence, or you might want to do a spell to make your superiors see your value and worth.

On the other hand, if the answer to your question is No, you will want to further investigate the circumstances that may be surrounding you at this time. If these are negative vibrations created by yourself or others, then you will want to do a ritual to negate them.

The Tarot can also be used as the focal point of a magickal rite or spell. For example, you might want to build a spell around the Lovers for developing a stronger relationship with your partner. Or you could use the Emperor to help improve your ability to make decisions and become a better leader.

When using a Tarot card as the focal point of a ritual, try to incorporate some of the symbolism of the card into the work. Choose candles that match the predominate color scheme of the card, and incorporate the card's meaning into your ritual liturgy. To reinforce the outcome of the ritual, use the card in meditation or post the card in a prominent place where you will be able to view it on a regular basis. The constant attention adds energy and power to the work.

9

The Moon and Magick

> "The moon is fundamental to any ritual work.
> It is the essence of mystery, magic, and mayhem."
> —Susan Bowes, *Life Magic*

The moon holds a special place in magickal lore, and like the sun, appears to rise in the East and set in the West. Unlike the sun, however, the appearance of its size and shape continually change. There are four cycles of approximately seven days each in a lunar month. The phases the moon goes through begin with the *Dark of the Moon* (also called the *New Moon*). It waxes and grows larger until the *first quarter* is visible as the Half Moon. When the moon waxes, or grows larger, its horns point to the West until it reaches a full circle known as the Full Moon. It will then begin to diminish in size as it wanes through the *last quarter* with the horns pointing East.

Dark (New)	First Quarter	Full	Last Quarter
●	☽	○	☾

Reflecting the light of the sun, the moon draws up the tides through her gravitational pull. It is this pull that affects human behavior. Since our bodies are about 65 percent water, we are naturally drawn to the movement of the lunar tides. When the moon is in her full pregnant glory, our dreams are more vivid, energies are higher, and psychic abilities are at their peak. Because of this, most Wiccans plan their rituals so they coincide with the movements of the moon.

Knowing the phases of the moon, and how to use them, will enhance your spells and magickal rites. Since most rituals work best when they are in agreement with corresponding planetary energies, it is important to time your magickal operations according to the phases of the moon. By doing this, you stay in synch with the forces of the universe, and combine natural outside energy and power with your own. When doing magick, the more circumstances you can bring into harmony with what you are doing, the better the results will be.

By taking the phases of the moon one at time, we see an inherent working pattern evolve. The period from the New Moon through the first quarter is usually referred to as the Waxing Moon. This is a time of new beginnings, initiating new projects, or beginning an adventure. Symbolically this is the Goddess's virgin aspect, and is attributed to the intellect and inspiration.

During the Full Moon, projects already begun are energized, nurtured, and reaffirmed. This phase of the moon relates to the Mother Goddess aspect—when psychic abilities and intuition are at their peak. This is the time of dreams, divination, and magickal rites that involve love, passion, and healing.

During the last quarter to Dark Moon is a time of contemplation, reflection, and banishing. It is associated with the Crone aspect of the Goddess. This is a good time to shed those extra pounds, get rid of debt, or banish an illness. Use the Dark Moon to cleanse and purify your surroundings. Let go of petty judgments and hatreds. By getting rid of what is of no longer any use, you are able to start fresh with the New Moon.

There are many ways to work with the different phases of the moon. I like to begin with the Dark Moon (the time just before New Moon), and use it to get rid of negative energies that may surround me or my goal. Then, when the New Moon arrives, I am able to begin working on something positive, without the influence of unwanted vibrations. I will then use the Full Moon to emphasize and reaffirm that which I have already set in motion. Finally, the Last Quarter is used for contemplation and gives the goal time to manifest.

THE LUNAR CALENDAR

In addition to the phases of the moon, each Full Moon of the month has a specific designation and symbolic meaning. Since early magickal practices were connected with hunting and agricultural processes, the Lunar Calendar reflects these themes. The significance of the seasonal moons may seem slightly antiquated, but this does not necessarily make them obsolete. Wicca is, after all, based on the early European fertility cults, and therefore reflects their priorities. Besides, energy is energy, and even though our ancestors may have used the phases of the moon and its energy for the procreation of the tribe or a bumper crop of corn, doesn't mean we can't use that same energy for intellectual and material endeavors.

MONTHLY FULL MOON ASSOCIATIONS

Because Wicca draws on a number of different folklore traditions and magickal systems, you will probably see different meanings assigned to the monthly Full Moons, depending upon what you read. One particular system's observances does not necessarily negate the other. Each arrangement has its own value and uses and it is up to the practitioner to pick the one that best suits their lifestyle. The following meanings are the ones most commonly used in Wicca today.

November (Snow Moon): This is the beginning of the dark season—the onset of winter. This is the time when the Earth resets, and all that resides upon it takes time to reflect. This is the season of death, and is a good time for divination, contemplation, and the releasing of negative thoughts and vibrations.

December (Oak Moon): The mighty oak withstands the cold hardship of winter. This is the time of hope and healing. The oak has long been revered because of its longevity, and the fact that such a mighty creature comes from the smallest acorn. December is a time to remain steadfast in convictions and principles as we look forward to the promise of the future.

January (Wolf Moon): The wolf has always been considered a fearsome creature of the night. It is a companion to the god of the hunt, and protector of the family. This moon occurs during the coldest and most desolate time of the year, a time when we look to the hearth and home for protection and comfort. It is both a time of endings and beginnings. Now is the time to reflect on the past and plan for the future.

February (Storm Moon): A storm is said to rage most fiercely just before it ends, and the year usually follows suit. The time of death and darkness are coming to an end, but there are still bleak, short days ahead. Now is time to plan for the future, face challenges, and break old habits.

March (Chaste Moon): The end of winter, and the beginning of spring brings forth new beginnings and a time of purity and newness. Everything has been made new again. The uncertainty of winter is behind us, and now we can plant the seeds of desire, fashion new goals, and prepare for new experiences.

April (Seed Moon): Spring is in the air and the seed moon signals the time of fertility and growth. This is the time to move from the planning phase into action. During the spring and early summer months you will need to nurture and empower your goals. If you are planning a garden filled with herbs and flowers that will be used for magickal purpose, now is the time to physically begin to plant.

May (Hare Moon): The hare was sacred to the Goddess, springtime, and fertility. By May all life is blossoming forth. Beltane, May Day, and romance are in the air. Passions run high. This is a great time to plant the last seeds that have been blessed and empowered with your desires. Take time to reaffirm your goals and intentions, nurture what has already been set into motion.

June (Dyad Moon): Dyad is the Latin name for pair—the twin stars of Castor and Pollux that exemplify the Gemini twins. This is a time of equality, union of opposites, and duality. It is a good time to reexamine your goals and actions. Physical energy is at its peak and emotions turn toward romance and marriage. This is also a good month for travel and the beginning of new partnerships.

July (Mead Moon): Mead was the traditional beverage of our European ancestors. This was a time for working to preserve some of those crops (mostly for wine and ale making) for winter and future use. It is the time to plan what you will do when you reach your goals. This is also a time of enchantment, strength, and renewed health.

August (Wyrt or Wort Moon): Wyrt is the Anglo Saxon term for herb or green plant. This is the first harvest—a time to celebrate and harvest the rewards of your labors. However, this is not the last or greatest harvest. There is still work to be done and the time of abundance and true success is still to come. If you have not reached your goal, you will need to put all your effort and focus your attention on it at this time. Plans for preserving what we have attained should be considered.

September (Barley Moon): We enter the sign of Virgo, the virgin who carries sheaves of barley and grain. This is the Great Harvest and in some circles the Harvest Moon. This is a time for celebration and realization of desired goals. This is also the time of the year when the grains are being harvested and is an excellent time for magick concerning abundance and success. Seek out that higher paying job. If you need to make a move, do it now before the energy begins to wane.

October (Blood Moon): This moon marked the season of hunting and the slaughter of the animals for winter food and clothing—animals that would not make it through the long winter months. Death surrounds us. The season of green has come to an end and the icy fingers of winter lurk on the horizon. When death is in the air it is believed that the veil between the worlds grows thin. This is a good time for divination, reflection, and preparation. What has been will now pass on, and what remains will need to be protected. Offerings of red wine, grain, and meat are left in a gesture of thanksgiving for all that has been received.

The Blue Moon: More than likely you have heard the expression "once in a blue moon," and, though it is commonly used, many people do not know what it means. The blue moon, is the second full moon in a calendar month. Since the Moon's cycle is twenty-nine-and-a-half days and some months have thirty-one days in them, you sometimes see a second full moon in the month. This does not happen often. In fact, it only occurs about every two and a half years. Like all unusual occurrences, the blue moon is a time of high energy. Most Wiccans save this time for really special magickal works. The Blue Moon is seen as an "extra" moon and a luxury. It is a good time to work for money, love, and personal success.

A Full Moon Ritual

Check your astrological calendar or *The Old Farmers Almanack* for the date and time of the next Full Moon. Use the ritual checklist to draft your ritual and inventory the items you will be using. For the standard Full Moon rite you will need the following items:

- Two white altar candles
- One white or silver pillar candle to represent the Moon and/or Goddess
- Athame or wand
- Chalice
- Pentacle
- Censer and incense
- Wine (or fruit juice)
- Bowl of water
- Bowl of salt

1. Consecrate the elements, cast the circle, and call in the Guardians.

2. Light the two white altar candles. Begin with the right one and say:

   With this light I bring truth and illumination to this sacred space.

   Light the left candle and say:

   With this light I bring reason and wisdom to this sacred space.

3. Pick up the censer, add incense, and walk to the East. Hold the incense in offering as you say:

   I offer the element of Air, for insight and wisdom.

Return the censer to the altar, pick up the right candle, and proceed to the South. Hold the candle in offering as you say:

I offer the element of Fire, for passion and power.

Return the athame to the altar, pick up the bowl of water, and go to the West. Hold the bowl in offering as you say:

I offer the element of Water, for control and dominion.

Return the bowl to the altar, pick up the bowl of salt, and go to the North. Hold the bowl in offering as you say:

I offer the element of Earth, for the manifestation of desire.

4. Return the bowl of salt to the altar. Light the silver or white candle and hold it in offering as you say:

   Lady who rules the stars and gods
      Mother of selfless devotion
   Enchantress of the mysteries
      And Keeper of time and motion.
   I light the way and invite thee here
      O Mother of sacred Earth
   Whose power is beyond compare
      I beseech thee to my dreams give birth.

5. At this point your sacred space has been set and the energy of the Goddess and the Moon have been summoned. You will want to use this time for your magickal work. Should you not have anything special that you are working toward, you can use this time for mediation, contemplation on future workings, or thanksgiving for those blessings you have already received.

6. When you have completed your ritual work you will want to preform the solitary Rite of Union. Pick up the chalice, hold it in offering, and say the following:

My Lord is the power and force of all life,
My Lady is the vessel through which all life flows.
My Lord is life and death,
My Lady is birth and renewal.
The sun brings forth life,
The moon holds it in darkness.

Place the chalice back on the altar. Pick up the athame, plunge it into the chalice as you say:

For as the Lance is to the male,
So the Grail is to the female,
And together they are conjoined to become one
In truth, power, and wisdom.

7. Begin the closing of your ceremony by extinguishing the altar candles, starting with the left one. Snuff out the candle as you say:

Let now the power, potential and force
    Return unto the original source.

Extinguish the right candle as you say:

Let now the motion, direction and sight
    Return unto the original light.

9. Dismiss the Guardians, and take up the circle. The rite has ended. At this time you should put all your tools and items away. Of course, if you have a room or area that has been set aside for ritual work you will only need to dismiss the Guardians and take up the circle.

SUGGESTIONS FOR WORKING WITH THE FULL MOON

Your full moon rituals do not have to be elaborate or complicated events. In most cases the previous ritual will suffice to personalize the ritual focus on the monthly moon you will be working with.

For example, if you are doing the Seed Moon (April) you might want to consider blessing a package of seeds. Compose a simple poem or chant and use this to energize the seeds, such as,

> *Blessed Be These Seeds*
> *That Will Satisfy My Needs.*

Along with blessing the seeds, decorate a special pot. Write on the pot what you want the seeds to represent—success, more money, or a better paying job. Fill the pot with earth and place it on your altar. Once you have blessed the seeds you can then plant them in the pot. By doing this you infuse the seeds and the earth with the energy from the circle and your ritual. Each time you water your seeds and then the plants, you reaffirm your desire and put magickal energy into your goal.

More Ideas and Symbolic Suggestions

Each Full Moon ritual, or magickal rite, you perform will have certain symbols that make the ceremony special. It is the symbols that help raise the level of consciousness, that in turn directs and focuses your energy toward the desired goal. The following suggestions can be used in conjunction with your Full Moon rites or for individual magickal works.

Love and Happiness

Spring brings forth fertility, love, and happiness. The full moons that fall during March, April, May, are best suited for attracting love and marriage. They can also be used to enhance partnerships and increase passion.

To help create the vibration you want, you can use: Rose quartz stones; pink or rose colored candles; rose, cherry, or apple blossom incense; heart shapes; lace fans and pearls; pink or red colored ink; strawberries; peaches; eggs.

Money and Prosperity

Take advantage of the seasons of the sun in June, July, and August to work on money, prosperity, and personal success projects.

The following items could be helpful: topaz, citrine, cat's eye stones; gold, yellow, or orange candles; gold coins; dollar bills; gold glitter; marigolds; honeysuckle incense; amber; pentacle.

Protection and Personal Power

Use the fall and the harvest moons of September, October, and November to rebuild personal strength and to protect what has been acquired during the year. It is of no use to acquire things only to loose them to another.

You can use: bloodstone and garnet stones; red, black, or brown candles; mirrors; Dragon's Blood incense; cinnamon; red carnations; snakes; athame, sword, or any weapons; fire.

Prophecy and Psychic Power

The winter months of December, January, and February are best suited for divination, increasing psychic powers, and planning for the future. Use the Full Moons to reflect on the past, and discover what the future holds.

You might wish to use: amethyst and lapis lazuli; blue or silver candles; gardenias, violets; Tarot cards or a crystal ball; galangal oil; wind instruments; bells; wand; lavender incense.

Wicca, Seasonal Rites, and Magick

> "Seasonal rites are literally as old as the hills
> on which they were once practiced by most of humanity.
> Periodically, in accordance with the natural tides
> of nature and the times indicated by the sun and
> moon, people came together to make dedicated
> representations of the things that bound them
> closest to the cosmic wheel of life."
> —William G. Gray, *Seasonal Occult Rituals*

The easiest and most efficient way to use magick is through the natural flow of the universe. One way this can be accomplished is through an alignment with the vibrational sequence of the seasons. This alignment brings us into contact with the forces of nature, as well as those energy forms represented by the God and the Goddess—the masculine and feminine forces of the universe.

In Wicca, the seasons are traditionally grouped into two categories, the Greater and Lesser Sabbats. The Greater Sabbats are

Imbolg, Beltane, Lughnasadh, and Samhain. The Lesser Sabbats occur on the two equinoxes and solstices. These Sabbats are often referred to as "Great Days" and provide us with a time to meet and celebrate our religion with those of like minds.

The Sabbats occur approximately every six weeks beginning with Samhain on October 31. To the magickally inclined, these Sabbats are not just a change of season and weather, but are a reflection of the life cycle processes of birth, life, and death. These special times of power allow us to align our natures with the essential energy behind all of creation to enhance magickal thought-forms—those dreams and desires we want to manifest into reality.

There are several ways of looking at Sabbats in connection with magick. One is through classical myths regarding the Lord of life and death uniting with the Lady of birth and renewal. Another is through ballads, in which stories like "John Barley Corn" explain the cycles of life through a series of poetic verses. And, since Wicca is a fertility-based philosophy, agricultural illustrations are probably the simplest way to demonstrate the power and potential of the Sabbats.

Using agriculture as our example, we view the seasons in terms of planning, planting, harvesting, and resting. As the last vestiges of snow and winter recede, the farmer plans his or her crop. With the first buds of spring, he or she will physically plant the seeds that will provide food in the months ahead. During the summer, those crops are nurtured and cared for. With the approach of fall, the crops are harvested, and the food preserved for the winter months. The ground will then lay fallow, life recedes, and all of nature takes time to rest and regenerate.

Though most of us are not farmers, and probably the closest we get to the actual crop is in the grocery store, we can still appreciate the farmer's simple, natural approach toward the work at hand. You never see a farmer out in the field in August trying to plant a new crop. Even if he or she were able to get the seeds to germinate, the frost in six weeks would kill the small delicate plants. Magick is the same—if we plan and plant the seeds of our desires at the appropriate times, then they will surely manifest. On the other hand, if we attempt to work in opposition to the natural flow then the rewards of our labors will be slim or nonexistent.

Magickally, the Sabbats provide a natural time frame for planning and working toward long-term goals. During the winter months we think about what needs to be done and formulate a plan of action. In the spring we take action, and physically as well as mentally plant the seeds of our desire. During the summer months we nurture and attend to the plants that symbolize our goal. With the coming of fall we are then ready to harvest the fruits of our labors, and receive the rewards for a job well done.

Since each Sabbat has a specific implication, and corresponding symbolic associations, they are an ideal way to focus energy toward a specific goal. By using the natural energies the Sabbats are aligned with, we add power and energy to our magickal works. For example, if you were trying to get a job promotion, you would plan out how to impress your boss during Yule. At Imbolg, you would use candle magick to give light to the work. At the Vernal Equinox, you would bless and plant seeds that represented your desire. During Beltane and Summer Solstice, you would nurture and water your plants and focus your intent. During Lughnasadh, you would bless the first of your harvest and focus your attention on impressing the boss with your capabilities. At the Autumn Equinox, you would give thanks for a bountiful harvest and for receiving your job promotion. With the onset of winter and Samhain, you would want to seek advice through divination on how to protect and maintain your new position.

I have provided a ritual that can be done during each of the Sabbats. They were designed for solitary practice, but can easily be used for celebration by a group. If you are planning to work with others, you will need to make copies of the ritual for each participant, and assign speaking parts prior to performing the rite. The person(s) conducting the ritual should know how to consecrate the elements, cast the circle, and the proper way to summon the Guardians. He or she should also be able to invoke the God and Goddess from memory as well as be able to bless the wine and cakes. For those just beginning, the invocations of the God and Goddess as well as the blessing of the wine and cake are included in Appendix I. If you have your own invocations and blessings, you may substitute them for the ones offered here.

THE EIGHT WICCAN SABBATS

YULE OR WINTER SOLSTICE

Yule is a pre-Christian holiday or festival that is celebrated on the Winter Solstice around the 21 of December. It is the true New Year, both astronomically as well as spiritually. At this time we see the simultaneous death and rebirth of the Sun God represented in the shortest day and longest night of the year. From this time forward, the sun grows in power and strength. To our ancestors, from where our teachings come, fertility was an important aspect of daily life. As the sun is vital to the concept of growth and fertility it is only natural that its return was celebrated with elaborate rituals and ceremonies. Though we don't necessarily use the Sabbat rites for fertility in a physical sense, the energy is still there and can be tapped into.

Yule is the time to think about what you want to accomplish, and outline the goal you wish to work toward. Magickally, you will want to make a talisman expressing your desires. This should be made using seasonal symbols. You might want to write your desire on a gift tag and place it inside of a plastic tree ornament that has been filled with pine, bay, and holly leaves. You can then place this talisman on your altar.

A RITUAL FOR YULE

Items needed: Cover the altar with a red cloth. On top of the altar place two red candles, your magickal tools, salt and water bowls for consecrating space, seasonal incense, one large red pillar candle, red and white wine, and cakes for blessing. At each Quadrant place the following candles: East–blue, South–red, West–green, North–yellow.

Begin the ritual by lighting the two altar candles, first the right one and then the left one as you say:

> *I light the fire of faith to illuminate the night*
> *I light the fire of hope to bring forth life.*

Then face the altar and say:

> *I call upon the white goddess*
> *And the sacrificed king*
> *To bless my works and deeds.*

Next, light the Quadrant candles. Begin in the East and say:

> *Lady of the whirling winds, host of the rising sun,*
>   *Guardian of light, be with me now.*

Move to the South, light the candle, and say:

> *Lord of fire and flame, host of the mid-day sun, Guardian*
>   *of life, be with me now.*

Proceed to the West, light the candle, and say:

> *Lady of the ocean tides, host of the setting sun, Guardian*
>   *of wisdom, be with me now.*

Go to the North, light the candle, and say:

> *Lord of the fields, host of the midnight sun, Guardian*
>   *of the ages, be with me now.*

Return to the altar and consecrate the elements, cast the magickal circle, and call in the Guardians of the four Quadrants.

Facing the altar invoke the God and then the Goddess.
Light the red pillar candle as you say:

> *Desolate and dormant is the earth above, and fertile is the*
> *soil below*
> *I pray that through this death dark cold, the way to light*
> *you will show.*
> *Bless now my works, my thoughts and deeds, and all that I*
> *have done*
> *Let now renewal and the way of life return with the glory*
> *of the sun.*
> *So Mote It Be.*

Next, pick up the talisman and speak the following blessing
over it:

> *Lord and Lady of the night*
> *Of the mist and the moonlight*
> *Bless now my thoughts, works and deeds*
> *That shall fulfill my wishes and needs.*
> *So Mote It Be.*

This is your personal time to meditate on the meaning of the
season and your goal. If you have a personal prayer or blessing
you would like to make, do it during this period of reflection.

Bless the wine and the cakes using your own words or those in
Appendix I.

Extinguish the Quadrant candles beginning with the North, and
saying:

> *Lord of the fields, host of the midnight sun, Guardian of*
> *the ages, I thank thee for thy blessings.*

Proceed to the West, extinguish the candle and say:

> *Lady of the ocean tides, host of the setting sun, Guardian*
> *of wisdom, I thank thee for thy blessings.*

Move to the South, extinguish the candle and say:

Lord of fire and flame, host of the mid-day sun, Guardian of life, I thank thee for thy blessings.

Go to the East, extinguish the candle and say:

Lady of the whirling winds, host of the rising sun, Guardian of light, I thank thee for thy blessings.

Dismiss the Guardians. Begin in the North and move widdershins ending with the East. Take up the circle in the same widdershins manner. You may now extinguish any additional candles that have been left to burn, take down the altar, and put all your tools away.

IMBOLG

Imbolg also known as Oimele or Brigantia, is celebrated on February 1. This is the feast of the waxing light or feast of lights, and is ascribed to the Goddess Bridget or Bride. This Sabbat is associated with the return of life and light and marks the awakening of the earth, the promise of spring and new beginnings.

The Eleusinian Mysteries held a torchlight procession on February 1 in honor of Demeter when she searched for her lost daughter Persephone that brought light back to the world when she was found. This is also the time of the Virgin–Maiden aspect of the Goddess being courted by the young lord God. Their passion for each other is felt in the seasonal energy at this time. Close in relationship to Imbolg is the Christian festival of Candlemas that is celebrated on February 2, and is considered to be a time of purification.

Now is when you want to prepare for what you wish to accomplish in the months to come. You should use this time to clarify and refine what you began at Yule. Since this is a festival of lights you will use a candle whose color, size, and shape best reflects your goal. This candle will be blessed and energized during the ritual, and should then be burned on a daily basis until the Vernal Equinox.

A Ritual for Imbolg

Items needed: Cover the altar with a white cloth. On top of the altar place two white or pink candles, your magickal tools, salt and water bowls for consecrating space, seasonal incense, one large white pillar candle, one personal candle for blessing, red and white wine, and cakes for blessing. At each Quadrant place the following candles: East–blue, South–red, West–green, North–yellow.

Begin the ritual by lighting the two altar candles, first the right one and then the left one as you say:

> *Gallant Lord, Protector, and Father of all, bring light, life, and wisdom.*
> *White Maiden, Gentle Mother, Silent One, Deliver me from ignorance and darkness.*

Next, light the Quadrant candles. Begin in the East and say:

> *I light the East to bring forth the dawn and the spirit of light.*

Move to the South, light the candle, and say:

> *I light the South to bring forth the power of the spirit of life.*

Proceed to the West, light the candle and say:

> *I light the West to bring forth passion and the spirit of love.*

Go to the North, light the candle and say:

> *I light the North to bring forth balance and the spirit of wisdom.*

Return to the altar, and consecrate the elements, cast the magickal circle, and then call in the Guardians of the four Quadrants.
Facing the altar, invoke the God and then the Goddess.
Now, light the white pillar candle as you say:

> With this light I welcome back the Spring
> That will bring life to every living thing.
> Let the glory of the gods I now behold
> Return what is given three fold.
> For as I revel in their presence and light
> I pray they will grant my needs this night.
>
> For out of death comes life
> Out of darkness comes light
> Out of winter comes Spring.

Using your athame, inscribe your name and your wish on the personal candle. Light the candle and place it in the center of the circle and say:

> My lady is the Goddess of fire,
> She rules the hearth, home and desire.
> Soon she shall visit as the Queen of Spring
> And bring forth life to every living thing.

This is your personal time to meditate on the meaning of the season and your goal. If you have a personal prayer or blessing you would like to make, do it during this period of reflection.
Bless the wine and the cakes using your own words or those in Appendix I.
Extinguish the Quadrant candles beginning in the North:

> Let the spirit of balance and wisdom be with me now.

Proceed to the West, extinguish the candle, and say:

> Let the spirit of passion and love be with me now.

Move to the South, extinguish the candle and say:

Let the spirit and power of life be with me now.

Go to the East, extinguish the candle, and say:

Let the spirit of the dawn and light be with me now.

Dismiss the Guardians. Begin in the North and move widdershins ending with the East. Take up the circle in the same widdershins manner. You may now extinguish any additional candles that have been left to burn, take down the altar, and put all your tools away.

THE VERNAL EQUINOX

Celebrated around March 21 this is the time when the sun crosses the plane of the Equator making the day and night of equal length. The Vernal Equinox is the actual beginning of spring and the agricultural season. We see many of the Christian Easter customs coming from this festive occasion including the ever popular practice of egg decorating. In ancient Egypt, Rome, and Greece, brightly colored eggs were eaten at this time as symbols of immortality, fertility, and resurrection.

The Vernal Equinox is considered to be a time of balance and harmony between the masculine and feminine forces of nature. This is also the time when we when we physically, as well as symbolically, plant the seeds of our desires—seeds that will grow into plants that represent our goal. You will want to choose seeds that represent your goal and bless them during this ritual.

A RITUAL FOR THE VERNAL EQUINOX

Items needed: Cover the altar with a lilac colored cloth. On top of the altar place two lilac colored candles, your magickal tools, salt and water bowls for consecrating space, seasonal incense, one large lilac pillar candle, a container of seeds for blessing, red and white wine, and cakes for blessing. At each Quadrant place the following candles: East–blue, South–red, West–green, North–yellow.

Begin the ritual by lighting the two altar candles, first the right one and then the left one as you say:

> *Lord of the Dark Realm descend*
> > *Move the spirit of my soul*
> *Renew within the vital force*
> > *Blend thy energies, make me whole.*

> *Lady of the Dark Realm come*
> > *Lead me into the new dawning day*
> *Protect me from the passions of man*
> > *Guide me along thy secret way.*

Next light the Quadrant candles. Begin in the East and say:

> *Blessed be the air of the eternal spirit, for it brings forth new beginnings.*

Move to the South, light the candle, and say:

> *Blessed be the fire of passion, for it brings forth power.*

Proceed to the West, light the candle, and say:

> *Blessed be the waters of regeneration, for they render rest and renewal.*

Go to the North, light the candle, and say:

> *Blessed be the earth of remembrance, for it provides hope and promise.*

Return to the altar and consecrate the elements, cast the magickal circle, and call in the Guardians of the four Quadrants.

Facing the altar, invoke the God and Goddess
Light the lilac candle as you say:

> *May the Lord and Lady of heaven and earth*
> *To life and spring now give birth*
> *At this time of equal night and equal light*
> *I pray you banish winters plight*
> *So Mote It Be.*

Pick up the package of seeds and chant the following over them. This will energize them with your desires.

> *Blessed be the seeds*
> *That satisfy my needs.*

This is your personal time to meditate on the meaning of the season and your goal. If you have a personal prayer or blessing you would like to make, do it during this period of reflection.

Bless the wine and cakes using your own words or those in Appendix I.

Extinguish the Quadrant candles beginning with the North and say:

> *Let the North always provide me with hope and promise.*

Proceed to the West, extinguish the candle, and say:

> *Let the West provide me with rest and regeneration.*

Move to the South, extinguish the candle, and say:

> *Let the South provide me with power and passion.*

Go to the East, extinguish the candle, and say:

> *Let the East provide me with insight and intuition.*

Dismiss the Guardians. Begin in the North and move widder-shins ending with the East. Take up the circle in the same widder-shins manner. You may now extinguish any additional candles that have been left to burn, take down the altar, and put all your tools away.

BELTANE

Celebrated on April 30, Beltane is primarily a fire and fertility fes-tival. Beltane, meaning "Bel-Fire," is derived from the Celtic god Bel, also known as Beli or Balor, which simply means Lord. Some seem to think that Bel was comparable to the Celtic Gaul god, Cernunnos. This is possible as most male gods relate to the sun and fire aspects.

Beltane is also the time of the May Queen in which a young woman was chosen from the village to represent the Earth God-dess and reflect the transformation of Maiden to Mother. This was also the time of the kindling of the "Need Fire," when all fires in the village were extinguished and then ritually relit the following day. Another ritual that was done at this time was to drive cattle through fires for purification and fumigation.

Fertility played an important role in the Beltane celebrations. The most significant symbol of this was the May Pole, also known as the axis mundi, around which (it was believed) the universe revolved. The pole personified masculine force and the disk at the top depicted the receptive female. There were seven colored rib-bons tied to the pole representing the seven colors of the rainbow.

On this night, we spiritually welcome back the Goddess in the form of the May Queen, and begin to actively pursue our goals on the material plane. Now is the time to take action and physi-cally put effort into your goals. Using a job promotion as an exam-ple, now would be the time to make your desires known to your supervisors. Let them see that you are both interested and capable of assuming more responsibility.

A Ritual for Beltane

Items needed: Cover the altar with a green colored cloth. On top of the altar place two green candles, a white taper candle, your magickal tools, salt and water bowls for consecrating space, seasonal incense, a large cauldron with a green candle in it should be placed in the center of the circle, red and white wine, and cakes for blessing. At each Quadrant place the following candles: East–blue, South–red, West–green, North–yellow.

Begin the ritual by lighting the two altar candles, first the right one, and then the left one as you say:

> *Let the darkness now give way to the light.*
> *Let the Lord and Lady bless this rite.*

Next, light the Quadrant candles. Begin in the East and say:

> *I light the East, the home of moonlight and consciousness.*

Move to the South, light the candle, and say:

> *I light the South, the home of fire and inspiration.*

Proceed to the West, light the candle, and say:

> *I light the West, the home of my watery beginnings.*

Go to the North, light the candle, and say:

> *I light the North, the home of all that is green and*
> *fruitful.*

Return to the altar and consecrate the elements, cast the magickal circle, and then call in the Guardians of the four Quadrants. Facing the altar invoke the God and Goddess.

Pick up the taper candle, light it, and say:

> *Let now the light of the creative spirit deliver me from*
> *darkness.*

Walk over to the cauldron and light the green candle inside it. With great emotion, speak the following blessing:

> *By the oak and by the stone,*
> > *Stands the cauldron of the Crone,*
> *Mistress of our birth and death*
> > *From who comes life's first breath,*
> *We approach your altar on this night*
> > *To summon forth thy sacred light,*
> *And all of those who dare to seek*
> > *Of your Mysteries we shall speak,*
> *With torch and flame this fire we fashion*
> > *To arouse your tempting passion,*
> *For you are the Maiden, Mother, and Wife*
> > *Whose triple will brings forth all life!*

This is your personal time to meditate on the meaning of the season and your goal. If you have a personal prayer or blessing you would like to make, do it during this period of reflection.

Bless the wine and cakes using your own words or those in Appendix I.

Extinguish the Quadrant candles beginning with the North, and say:

> *Let the abundance of the green Earth grant me prosperity.*

Proceed to the West, extinguish the candle, and say:

> *Let the tides of the great oceans grant me wisdom.*

Move to the South, extinguish the candle, and say:

> *Let the fire that falls from the sky grant me inspiration.*

Go to the East, extinguish the candle, and say:

> *Let the winds that approach from the East grant me insight.*

Dismiss the Guardians. Begin in the North and move widdershins ending with the East. Take up the circle in the same widdershins manner. You may now extinguish any additional candles that have been left to burn, however, do not extinguish the candle in the cauldron—allow it to burn out. Take down the altar, and put all of your tools away.

SUMMER SOLSTICE

Summer Solstice is celebrated around June 21. This is the longest day and shortest night of the year. The festival of the Summer Solstice is concerned with both fire and water. Our ancestors believed that fire would help keep the sun alive, and that it would soon decline from this point forward. All wells, springs, and bodies of water (considered the source of all life) were considered sacred and would be blessed at this time.

An ancient custom of our ancestors was the leaping over or passing through fires. It was believed that the higher a person jumped the higher the crops would grow. As with Beltane, cattle were driven through the fires for purification and fumigation. It was also believed that the fire repelled the powers of evil, and would protect all who passed through it.

Another symbol used at this time is that of the wheel. The turning of the wheel has long represented the turning or progression of the seasons. Wheels were decorated with flowers and lighted candles were placed on them. These wheels were then set afloat on the nearest body of water.

Symbolically, now is the time to nurture your goals or efforts. That which you have been working toward should now be within range. You will want to continue to care for and sustain your impending goal in every possible way.

A RITUAL FOR THE SUMMER SOLSTICE

Items needed: Cover the altar with a bright yellow cloth. On top of the altar place two yellow candles, a white taper candle, your magickal tools, salt and water bowls for consecrating space, seasonal incense, a floating candle in a large bowl of water should be placed on the center of the altar, red and white wine, and cakes for blessing. At each Quadrant place the following candles: East–blue, South–red, West–green, North–yellow.

Begin the ritual by lighting the two altar candles, first the right one, and then the left one as you say:

> Sacred is this time of equal day and equal night.
> Sacred is the summer sun that gives us life and light.

Next, light the Quadrant candles. Begin in the East and say:

> Let the East, the winds of consciousness, bring forth new light.

Move to the South, light the candle, and say:

> Let the South, the fires of motivation, bring forth the
> blazing sun.

Proceed to the West, light the candle, and say:

> Let the West, the waters of passion, hold back the twilight.

Go to the North, light the candle, and say:

> Let the North, the home the fertile earth, always return
> from darkness.

Return to the altar and consecrate the elements, cast the magickal circle, and call in the Guardians of the four Quadrants.

Facing the altar, invoke the God and Goddess.

Use the taper candle to light the floating candle as you say:

> The Lord of the fire, and the golden sphere
> Speaks to the Lady who now draws near
> And through the candle flame they speak
> Bringing wisdom and insight to all who seek

To understand the mystery within their power lies
The secret key that will allow all to rise
Above the limitations of this confined earth
And to our dreams and desires give birth.

Pick up the bowl with the floating candle in it and offer it to each Quadrant. Begin in the East and say:

The sun shall rise and bring wisdom for the spirit.

Move to the South and say:

The sun shall radiate and provide power for the spirit.

Proceed to the West and say:

The sun shall set and nourish the mystery of the spirit.

Go to the North and say:

The sun shall be reborn and make new the spirit.

Place the bowl in the center of the circle.

This is your personal time to meditate on the meaning of the season and your goal. If you have a personal prayer or blessing you would like to make, do it during this period of reflection.

Bless the wine and cakes using your own words or those in Appendix I.

Extinguish the Quadrant candles beginning with the North, and say:

Let now my desires manifest as the North returns to
darkness.

Proceed to the West, extinguish the candle and say:

Let now my passion bring forth completeness as the West
accepts the twilight.

Move to the South, extinguish the candle and say:

*Let now my actions motivate my awareness as the South
gives host to the sun.*

Go to the East, extinguish the candle and say:

*Let now my thoughts provide me with insight as the East
gives rise to the light.*

Dismiss the Guardians. Begin in the North and move widdershins ending with the East. Take up the circle in the same widdershins manner. You may now extinguish any additional candles that
have been left to burn, however, do not extinguish the candle in
the bowl—allow it to burn out. Take down the altar and put all of
your tools away.

LUGHNASADH OR LAMMAS

The festival of Lughnasadh (Celtic) or Lammas (Christian) is held
on August 1. The word *Lughnasadh* is associated with the god Lugh,
and the festival was held to commemorate his marriage. Lammas is
derived from the Old English *hlafmoesse*, meaning "loaf-mass," and
was held in celebration of the first loaves baked from the first grain
harvested. The loaves were taken to the local church, blessed by
the priest, and then distributed among the congregation. It was
believed that by observing this custom, abundance was ensured for
the coming Great Harvest at the Autumn Equinox.

Corn and grain are predominate features of rituals at this time
because they symbolize both fertility and abundance. The golden
ears of corn are seen as the offspring of the marriage between the
sun and virgin earth (the sky father and the earth mother). Corn
and grain, like bread and wine, symbolize humankind's labor and
the ability to sustain life.

This is the first harvest and the time we accept the *responsibility*
as well as *rewards* for our labors. At this time, your goal should be

in the early stages of physical manifestation. Continuing with the example of the job promotion, if all has gone according to plan, you should be in training for your new position.

A Ritual for Lughnasadh

Items needed: Cover the altar with an orange cloth. On top of the altar place two orange candles, your magickal tools, salt and water bowls for consecrating space, seasonal incense, a bundle of corn tied with orange ribbon should be placed on the center of the altar, red and white wine, and cakes for blessing. At each Quadrant place the following candles: East-blue, South-red, West-green, North-yellow.

Begin the ritual by lighting the two altar candles, first the right one, and then the left one as you say:

The sun brings forth light and the seed of life
The moon sustains the life and brings forth the grain.

Next, light the Quadrant candles. Begin in the East and say:

I call upon soft and whispering winds for intellect and perception.

Move to the South, light the candle, and say:

I call upon warm and quickening light for power and protection.

Proceed to the West, light the candle, and say:

I call upon cool and tranquil seas for control and dominion.

Go to the North, light the candle, and say:

I call upon flowering forest and field for beauty and pleasure.

Return to the altar and consecrate the elements, cast the magickal circle, and call in the Guardians of the four Quadrants.

Facing the altar invoke the God and Goddess.

Pick up the bundle of corn, hold it in offering as you say:

> *Corn and grain are of this earth*
> *With love and work I gave them birth*
> *Though they were once just small seeds*
> *They now will satisfy my needs*
> *And like the grain and like the corn*
> *I shall ever return and be reborn*
> *So Mote It Be.*

Place the corn in the center of the circle, and focus on your goal.
When you feel the time is right, chant the following to empower
the corn with your thought-form:

> *Corn and grain, bring joy and gain.*

This is your personal time to meditate on the meaning of the
season and your goal. If you have a personal prayer or blessing
you would like to make, do it during this period of reflection.

Bless the wine and cakes using your own words or those in
Appendix I.

Extinguish the Quadrant candles beginning with the North, and
say:

> *Flowering field and forest, bring forth great beauty and*
> *bounty.*

Proceed to the West, extinguish the candle and say:

> *Cool waters and gentle rain, bring forth love and*
> *compassion.*

Move to the South, extinguish the candle and say:

> *Warm and quickening light, bring forth strength and*
> *passion.*

Go to the East, extinguish the candle and say:

*Soft and whispering winds, bring forth insight and
wisdom.*

Dismiss the Guardians. Begin in the North and move widdershins ending with the East. Take up the circle in the same widdershins manner. You may now extinguish any additional candles that
have been left to burn. Take down the altar, and put all of your
tools away. Hang the corn so that it will dry, as you will need it to
make your corn-baba for the Autumnal Equinox.

THE AUTUMNAL EQUINOX

The Autumnal Equinox is a time of equal day and equal night and
is on or near September 21. From this night, the days grow shorter,
and the sun begins to wane in power. This is the last of the harvest
celebrations and is traditionally referred to as The Harvest Home,
the end of the agricultural year.

At this time all of the crops have been gathered, canning and stor-
age for the winter is a priority, and wine making is in full progress.

The purpose of the Autumnal Equinox is two-fold. First you
want to give thanks for what you have received, and second, you
want to project for the ability to maintain what we are in possession of. It is of no value to manifest a goal if you cannot keep it. To
aid in this process, you should fashion a corn-baba that represents

To make a corn-baba you will need to strip off the dried husks
from the corn cob you blessed at Lughnasadh. Soak them in
water until pliable. Use the cob as the body. Use paper, or a
cotton ball to form the head. Then cover with strips of husks
and attach to the cob with strings. Cut a narrow strip of husk
and roll into 7-inch length. Tie off the ends with string for
arms. Attach to the cob and then fashion a dress from any left-
over soaked husks. Use the silk or yellow yarn for hair.

thanksgiving, and the hope for the ability to keep what has been brought into being.

A Ritual for Autumnal Equinox

Items needed: Cover the altar with a brown cloth. On top of the altar place two brown candles, your magickal tools, salt and water bowls for consecrating space, seasonal incense, and a cornucopia filled with seasonal vegetables should be placed on a table in the center of the circle along with your corn-baba. You will need red and white wine, and cakes for blessing. At each Quadrant place the following candles: East–blue, South–red, West–green, North–yellow.

Begin the ritual by lighting the two altar candles, first the right one, and then the left one as you say:

> *Lord of the dark realm descend*
> *Your strength and power now lend*
> *Lady of the moon's bright light*
> *Impart your blessings on this night.*

Next, light the Quadrant candles. Begin with the East and say:

> *Equal day and equal night, cast away the shadows, bring*
> *in the light.*

Move to the South, light the candle, and say:

> *Flaming autumn fire, show me the way, to bring forth*
> *desire.*

Proceed to the West, light the candle, and say:

> *Reflections from the past, deep within, let your memories last.*

Go to the North, light the candle, and say:

> *The gathered crops, and barren land, reward the working*
> *hand.*

Return to the altar and consecrate the elements, cast the magickal circle, and call in the Guardians of the four Quadrants.

Facing the altar invoke the God and Goddess.

Now pick up the corn-baba and bless it, saying:

> *Hearty has been the harvest*
> *　　That was the work of my hand.*
> *It brought forth hope and promise*
> *　　From blessed and sacred land.*
> *I hold this sacred promise*
> *　　Let happiness fill my days*
> *For all the world to know and see*
> *　　The wisdom of these ways.*

Place the corn-baba on the table next to the cornucopia. When you feel the time is right, chant the following to empower the corn-baba:

> *Bless my every work and deed,*
> *　　That I shall never want or need.*

This is your personal time to meditate on the meaning of the season and your goal. If you have a personal prayer or blessing you would like to make, do it during this period of reflection.

Bless the wine and cakes using your own words or those in Appendix I.

Extinguish the Quadrant candles beginning with the North, and say:

> *Death is upon us and rebirth shall follow. The harvest*
> *　　provides.*

Proceed to the West, extinguish the candle, and say:

> *Now is the time of passing and reflected light. The harvest*
> *　　sustains.*

Move to the South, extinguish the candle, and say:

Autumn fires burn bright and kindle passions. The harvest preserves.

Go to the East, extinguish the candle, and say:

Shadows are cast and icy winds blow. The harvest prevails.

Dismiss the Guardians. Begin in the North and move widdershins ending with the East. Take up the circle in the same widdershins manner. You may now extinguish any additional candles that have been left to burn. Take down the altar, and put all of your tools away. The corn-baba should be hung over the main entrance of the home, and the cornucopia used for a table decoration during the harvest season.

SAMHAIN

Samhain pertains to Summer's End, and is celebrated on October 31. This is the end of the agricultural season and the beginning of the Wiccan New Year. Samhain is also the festival of the dead and was Christianized as All Souls or All Saints day. Samhain is traditionally a time of chaos, and the reversal of normal order due to the simultaneous aspects of ending and beginning.

For our early ancestors and the agricultural community, this was the time of year when the majority of the herd was butchered to provide food for the winter months. Slaughter, barren earth, and decreasing daylight made the concept of death an ever present reality. Because of this association with death, Samhain has always been considered a time when the veil between the worlds was thin–a night of magick charms and divination when the dead could be easily contacted.

On this night, through spiritual myth, we see the goddess of vegetation and growth return to the underworld. For now is the time of the Horned God of the hunt, the god of death and regeneration. It is He who will rule over the winter months—the time of transition when we switch from life to death.

On an individual basis this is the time to rest and re-evaluate our lives and goals. Now is when we want to get rid of any negativity or opposition that may surround our achievements or hinder future progress. At this point you have accomplished your desires and realized your goal. Now you will wan to stabilize and protect what has been gained. This is important because it is impossible to concentrate, let alone put energy, into new goals, if what we have is not secure. You will want to bind off any negative influences that may surround you with a protection talisman.

A RITUAL FOR SAMHAIN

Items needed: Cover the altar with a black cloth. On top of the altar place two black candles, a black taper, your magickal tools, salt and water bowls for consecrating space, seasonal incense, and a black cauldron with a red candle in it should be placed in the center of the circle. Set your talisman next to the cauldron. You will need red and white wine and cakes for blessing. At each Quadrant place the following candles: East-blue, South-red, West-green, North-yellow.

Begin the ritual by lighting the two altar candles, first the right one, and then the left one as you say:

> *Sacred is this time of death and regeneration*
> *Sacred is this time of transition and transformation.*

Next, light the Quadrant candles. Begin with the East, and say:

> *Let there be light in the East, the home of the eternal*
> *spirit.*

Move to the South, light the candle, and say:

> *Let there be light in the South, the home of the divine*
> *spark.*

Proceed to the West, light the candle, and say:

> Let there be light in the West, the home of rest and
> regeneration.

Go to the North, light the candle, and say:

> Let there be light in the North, the home of the final
> atonement.

Return to the altar and consecrate the elements, cast the mag-
ickal circle, and call in the Guardians of the four Quadrants.
Facing the altar invoke the God and Goddess.
Next, light the black taper and hold it in offering as you say:

> Blessed is the death Crone
>> And her silent tides of death and birth,
> For she alone brought love
>> Life and wisdom to our earth.
> Blessed is the dying king
>> And the sacrificed blood he shed,
> For he alone will guide us
>> Through the time of darkness and dread.

Using the black taper, light the candle inside the cauldron as
you say:

> In a place that is not a place
>> Within this consecrated space
> I bid farewell to my Lady dear
>> And pray she shall return next year.
> I welcome back the Lord of light
>> To protect me from this winters plight
>> So Mote It Be.

This is your personal time to meditate on the meaning of the
season and your goal. If you have a personal prayer or blessing
you would like to make, do it during this period of reflection.

Bless the wine and cakes using your own words or those in Appendix I.

Extinguish the Quadrant candles beginning with the North, and say:

> *Death now brings darkness to the North, the home of the final atonement.*

Proceed to the West, extinguish the candle and say:

> *Death now brings darkness to the West, the home of rest and regeneration.*

Move to the South, extinguish the candle and say:

> *Death now brings darkness to the South, the home of the divine spark.*

Go to the East, extinguish the candle and say:

> *Death now brings darkness to the East, the home of the eternal spirit.*

Dismiss the Guardians. Begin in the North and move widdershins ending with the East. Take up the circle in the same widdershins manner. You may now extinguish any additional candles that have been left to burn; however, the candle in the cauldron should be left to burn out. Take down the altar, and put all of your tools away.

11

Wiccan Magick and Spell-Crafting

"Spell craft may seem to be a new idea, but it's as old
as the day when a human first shaped a natural
object to fulfill a spiritual need."

—Scott Cunningham and David Harrington, *Spell Crafts*

Like any other form of magick, spells always work best when
properly performed, under controlled conditions. They also
allow you another form of expression and occasion to work
toward your desires. By taking advantage of the extra time between
Full Moons and Sabbats, you are able to reinforce and reaffirm
your goals.

Just what is a spell and how is it different from a ritual? A spell
is a *period of time* during which an object, person, or situation is
held in a captive state for the benefit of the person working his or
her will and intent. This is accomplished by selecting and using
words, music, or chants that have a dominating effect over the

recipient. Spells result in direct and dynamic effects, and usually get immediate results. On the other hand, a ritual is a *prescribed event or ceremony*, built up by tradition and repetition. Rituals must be repeated over a period of time to be effective, whereas most spells need only be done once in order to achieve results.

Unfortunately, there is a disadvantage to simple spellcasting that isn't present with ritual work. The drawback is in the quality and durability of the results. Spells act fast, and are easily and quickly done, but the results are not as long lasting as those of a formal magickal rite. However, there are those moments when something is needed in a hurry and there just isn't time for a formal rite. This is what spells were made for—immediate action and help with a problem.

Out of all magick, spellcasting is the easiest and most popular. Spells do not require any specific amount of room and can be done almost anywhere with a minimal amount of equipment. However, as with all magick, the art of spellcasting has its guidelines and rules. These are necessary for achieving effective results. The three major factors to consider before starting a spell are:

- Necessity,
- Proper ingredients, and
- Focused energy.

Necessity. What is it that you want, better yet, really need? How emotionally involved are you with your present desire or goal? Without the proper emotion and total involvement of focused energy the spell will not work. You don't just sit around casting spells for lack of anything else to do. Also, you—and only you— are totally responsible for what you do or don't do. It is not up to others to judge your secret desires, but it is up to you to attempt to fulfill them. You, and only you, can make yourself happy. No one else can do it for you. Other people can't make you happy, they just momentarily distract you from some desire or inner conflict.

Proper ingredients. This is where so many make the biggest mistake, not using the exact ingredients called for in a spell. Don't substitute if you don't have the *exact* items you need. Wait until you are able to get them. You can fool the ego, but not your higher self, and this is where your power comes from. Don't take short cuts. If the spell calls for marigolds, it doesn't mean basil. If the burning time for a candle is two hours, then it must burn for two hours not one hour and ten minutes because you have other things to do.

Focused energy. This is the personal power that you project because of an emotional tie with the objective. The need, desire, and total lustful involvement must be there or the energy level will not be high enough to cause a reaction. One hundred percent of your attention must be given at the moment of action; you must force your intent out and into the atmosphere. It is your personal power and energy that make a spell work. You can have all the right ingredients, but if the energy and enthusiasm are not there, this will be reflected in the results or lack thereof.

Spells, like rituals, require a certain amount of planning and preparation. If you are creating the spell yourself, then you will need to plan your spell so it will coincide with the proper phase of the Moon or planetary energy. The spell will also have to be arranged in a logical manner so as to accomplish what it is you wish in the least amount of time. You should make a checklist, as you do with a ritual, of all the items you will need or be using before you begin any spell. Following are some helpful hints and important points to remember when preparing for spell working.

SPELLCASTING TIPS

- Assemble all of the ingredients that will be used.
- Label each package of herbs, incense, and all oils with their contents and purpose.

- Put all of the items you will need together in a box or in a bag on or near your altar.
- If you need to do the spell several times, be sure to plan it so that you are able to repeat it at the same time every day.
- Be sure to read over the spell several times so that you know exactly what you will be doing.
- Try not to eat before working magick. It is best not to eat any dairy or meat products prior to the work. If you are able to, fast for at least least twelve hours prior to any magickal operation. It is also advisable to restrain from sexual activity for this period as well. Food, and especially sexual activity, grounds energy. The idea is to have all your energies at their peak for the work or rite. Once the ritual or spell has been completed, then you will want to ground your energies.

The Talisman

The word talisman means to consecrate. It is the process of consecration that converts the object you are using into an effective—*active*—magickal channel for working your will. It is best if the consecration process is part of the spell or magickal rite in which the talisman will be used.

The famous ceremonial magician, MacGregor Mathers, defined a talisman as "a magical figure charged with the force it is intended to represent." In other words, talismans are actively charged objects constructed to attain a definite result. It is not like an amulet that is generally used for bringing good luck or warding off evil. An efficient talisman should be capable of operating in such a way that its effectiveness is obvious immediately, or at least within seven days of its construction.

Talismans are easy and fun to work with. They can be made from just about anything and can be used to acquire money, obtain patronage, recover lost property, influence people, increase knowledge, disrupt friendships, charm someone to love you, and protect your property and loved ones.

Once the talisman has been created and charged, it can be left to do its work without further attention. This is because the energy setup at the time of the consecration continues to work over a set period of time. The talisman works like a battery and is self-recharging to some extent (if the construction has been carried out correctly). This ability to recharge, is due to the relationship between the talisman and its corresponding symbolic force.

THE AMULET

The amulet is an object that has been left in its virgin state, and is then psychically charged or energized with a specific purpose in mind. Amulets are usually used for protection as they are passive in their communicative abilities. Only when their barriers have been crossed do they react or retaliate. A good example would be the horseshoe over the door that brings luck to all who cross beneath it, or the protection amulet that wards off the negativity of others when they come in contact with it.

Almost any symbolic object can be turned into an amulet. Special stones, shells with markings, wood carvings, and statues—anything which already exists or is in a natural state—can be turned into an amulet simply by forcing your will and dynamic energy into it. Because of the amulet's passive nature, and the fact that most of its power resides in its intrinsic symbology, there is no need to formally consecrate it. Remember, amulets are passive, and their power resides in their natural symbology.

CANDLE MAGICK

Candles are automatically magickal as they bring light to the darkness. They are in themselves illumination, and represent the vitalizing power of the sun. Candles are a symbol of light—the individual soul. Just as the flame consumes the wax, so candles illustrate the relationship between spirit and matter.

Candles can be used by themselves as a form of magick, or may be incorporated as part of a spell. In either case, the candle itself becomes the point of focus. The color of the candle, its shape and size all play an important role in the art of candle magick. The color signifies the intent, the design or shape represents the objective, and the size is equivalent to the amount of time needed for burning.

Burning time frame (how long a candle should burn) is as essential to candle magick as color is. Each color of the spectrum has its own special wavelength or vibrational frequency. This vibrational frequency is the equivalent of motion and energy, which is the amount of time needed to activate the spell. Therefore, a candle that takes four hours to burn will take four times longer to work than a candle that only requires one hour to burn. I've included a list of candle color magick correspondences for a handy reference guide.

In addition to their difference in color, candles also come in a variety of shapes other than the simple household taper. There are image candles in the shape of men and women, animal shapes such as a cat, and even ones that come shaped like the human hand and skull. Use symbolic candles when you want to add extra energy to your spell. Since they already represent a specific idea, they will enhance your ability to focus your attention and energy toward your goal.

How to Energize the Candle (Candle Dressing)

The first step is to choose a candle by color or shape that represents your desire. Next you will have to dress the candle. This is done by anointing the entire candle with a special oil that usually represents your desire as well. Place some of the oil on your fingertips, and as you concentrate on your desire rub the oil onto the candle, begin-

Color Magick Correspondences

Color	Color Meaning	Burning Time
Red	Courage, strength, immediate action, survival, lust, and power	One hour
Pink	Love, friendship, calm, emotions	One hour
Orange	Action, attraction, selling, self-promotion	Two hours
Yellow	Communication, selling persuasion, attraction	Three hours
Green	Love, fertility, money, luck, health, personal goals	Four hours
Blue	Creativity, tranquility, peace, perception, patience	Three hours
Dark blue	Wisdom, self-awareness, psychic abilities, to cause change	Two hours
Purple	Power, ambition, tension, spiritual development, power over others	One hour
Black	Protection, return, cause discord, release negativity, power	One hour
Brown	Stability, grounding, earth rites, to create indecision	Four hours
Gold	Prosperity, attraction, increase wealth, money drawing	One hour
White	Universal color, general candle magick	No set time

ning from the center upwards, and then from the center downward (as pictured). Be sure to cover the entire candle with the oil.

When you are planning a candle magick spell, try to keep all of your symbolism or vibrations the same. For example, if you were doing a love spell you would want to use a red image candle and love drawing oil. If you were trying to open up the lines of communication between you and another person you might want to try a yellow candle and mercury oil. For a peaceful home, use a blue candle, tranquility oil, and maybe some sandalwood incense. The whole idea is to keep your colors, objects, and thoughts similar in meaning and symbology. By doing this your energy is focused for maximum effect. Also, when special oils are not available, you can always use a good quality olive oil.

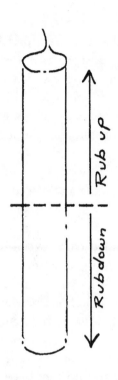

SYMBOLIC OBJECTS

Effective magick hinges upon the relationship between emotion and expressed energy. Symbols create automatic responses to people, places, and situations. It is this response coupled with directed emotion, that creates the desired outcome. The wonderful thing about most magickal works, especially spellcasting, is that almost any ordinary object can serve as the response trigger.

For example, how many times have you picked up a doll or stuffed toy and remarked on how much it looked like someone you knew? Other objects include a photograph of a loved one that creates an instant emotional response, a painting in the museum that triggers a past life experience, or a statue in a garden that almost seems if it will speak with you. These may seem like ordinary objects to others, but they bring out special feelings and emotions in you. This is what magick is all about—triggering emotions—bringing feelings to the surface so their energy can be focused and directed toward a desired outcome.

It doesn't take much imagination to find symbolic objects: a picture or figure of a dragon might be turned into a protective amulet and placed near the door; the ordinary household broom, once activated and charged, can be used to clear negative vibrations and energies from the room; small heart-shaped pillows, filled with special herbs, make wonderful love-drawing amulets. Almost any box or bag can be turned into a talisman by adding special stones, a picture, herbs, and magickal sigils. In fact, most Wiccan households are one giant magickal talisman from the front door to the back. About the only thing one notices different about the Wiccan household is the peace and tranquility they feel while there. For the most part, magick is a practical way to reach your goals. It is not to be abused nor is it to be feared. It is just another process of getting what you want.

Wicca and the Qabalah

"There is a tree that has its roots in heaven. . . . A tree
that contains all that is, and was, and will be, and might
be, and could be. It contains a kingdom, a foundation,
glory, victory, beauty, might, mercy, understanding,
wisdom . . . and a crown."

—Ellen Cannon Reed, *The Witches Qabala*

The Qabalah, is considered by some to be the cornerstone of magick, especially those older and more established in Wiccan traditions. If you can look past its seemingly patriarchal overtones, and complex designs, you find a magickal system that readily fits into Wicca. Gardnerian, Alexandrian, and Hermetic traditions all incorporate the Qabalah into their teachings and magickal rites—believing that it helps train the mind for spiritual work.

The Qabalah is like a map of the soul. There are twenty-two paths that travel between ten spheres called Sephiroth (emanations or spheres of light). These paths and spheres provide a detailed plan to follow in order to attain various levels of consciousness. The spheres and paths are arranged in a pattern that is called the "Tree of Life," which is filled with a myriad of gods,

The Myth

In the beginning there was a garden. One day a serpent (the bad guy) appeared in the garden and told the innocent humans, who occupied the garden, they would, "become as the Gods" if they ate of the forbidden fruit, so they did. This upset the Lord God (the good guy), who grumpily agreed after the fact that "Man had become like the gods, and now knew the difference between good and evil." Obviously, the wrong thing to do. So this same Lord God kicked the disobedient humans out of the Garden of Eden before they could commit the ultimate transgression and partake of the Tree of Life that would grant them everlasting life. Then, God posted Kerubims (a type of winged-bull angel) armed with flame-throwers at the Gate to the Garden, to keep the humans from sneaking back in when he wasn't looking. From that moment on, the seeking of the fruit of the Tree of Life has became a quest, like that of seeking the Holy Grail. It it is believed that once either is acquired, the discoverer becomes as the Gods—all knowing and without end.

goddesses, angelic forms, and wisdom—spiritual wisdom that will enhance life.

Unfortunately, there is no way to broach the study of the Qabalah in just one chapter. Since the Qabalah offers such a vast and comprehensive method of classifying the universe, in terms of both macrocosm and microcosm, it takes time to truly learn it. To use the Qabalah effectively, you must learn to move within its spheres where its true mystical experience awaits, but this takes years of study. I am providing merely an introduction to the Qabalah. Should it whet your appetite, there are literally hundreds of books available on the Qabalah and related magickal paths.

The Qabalah is a Jewish doctrine or system of theosophy that explains the importance of humanity's role in God's universe. The primary application of the Qabalah is spiritual advancement, attained through a concentrated study of the Tree of Life and specific God names. In the practice of ceremonial magick, knowledge of the Qabalah is applied without fail, particularly in the making and consecrating of amulets and talismans.

The word Qabalah comes from the Hebrew word *QBL* (Qoph Beth Lamed) and means "to receive." Allegedly, the Qabalah was given to the Hebrew scholars by an archangel to help them understand the Mysteries, so they could help others experience them. Supposedly, only the glyph for the Tree of Life, and the Names of Power were given, all else was added later as the system grew in importance and popularity.

During the first few centuries after Christ, when the Church was growing, the Jewish religion as all non-Christian faiths, was considered Pagan and forced underground. No doubt there was a great sharing of knowledge between the Jewish scholars and those of other mystical traditions. During this period the Qabalah began to really grow and develop. Planetary attributes, gods and goddesses, the Major Arcana of the Tarot, and the elements were eventually all added to the Tree of Life.

Even though there is no agreement on the actual origin of the Qabalah, there is agreement that its basis is from the *Sepher Yetzirah* (Book of Formation) by an anonymous author. *The Sepher Yetzirah* deals with the creation of the universe by means of ten Sephiroth. These Sephiroth are equated with the archetypal numbers one through ten, and the twenty-two letters of the Hebrew alphabet. Together, the numbers and the letters form what is commonly held to be the "thirty-two paths of wisdom." expressed through the Tree of Life glyph.

Essentially, the Qabalah is the search for God, or ultimate identity, using a system of mathematically connected concepts that are rational and logical. The modern Qabalah is based on Hebrew

principles that come from sources related to those that wrote the
Bible. However, the Qabalah is not a religion, but rather a *way of
working* with the inner principles of life—the powers that be—in
terms of values that apply to everyday awareness. Through study of
the Qabalah the practitioner is able to develop an affinity with
God as he or she progresses upon the thirty-two paths of wisdom
and Tree of Life.

It is said that the Tree of Life has it roots in heaven, and contains
all that is, all that was, all that will be, and all that could be. It con-

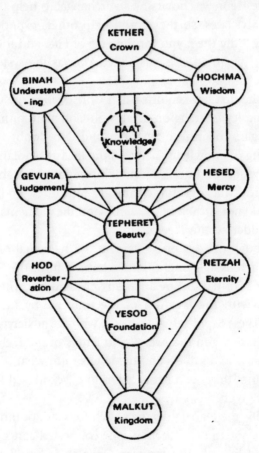

Tree of Life

tains the kingdom, foundation, glory, victory, beauty, might, mercy, understanding, wisdom, and a crown. On it are observations that when properly applied, bring specific spiritual experiences and revelations. The Tree also shows how God created the universe through a lightning flash that extended from the first Sephiroth to the tenth Sephiroth. In addition, by ascending the Tree through specific meditations one is able to work their way back to God.

THE SEPHIROTH

- Kether (The Crown) is the creative stage, and is operated by the Archangel Metatron. It is the reunion with the original source. The magickal image here is an ancient bearded king seen in profile. This the realm of attainment, and completion of the Great Work.
- Chokmah (Wisdom) is the crown of creation. This Sephiroth is considered to be the second glory. The Archangel Ratzkiel maintains this sphere of light. Here is where God is said to proclaim the secrets of the universe.
- Binah (Understanding) is the feminine aspect of Divinity whose intuitive awareness makes up the other half of an omniscient deity. Tzafkiel, the watcher of God, takes care of this Sephiroth.
- The Abyss (Abbadon) presides over lost souls and causes. It is Masak Mavdil or place for rejected failures. Through the Abyss everything and anyone who was useless to life had to be recycled.
- Chesed (Mercy) is the cohesive or receptive intelligence. This Sephiroth is controlled by the Archangel Tzadkiel whose name means "the righteous of God." This Sephiroth represents the benevolent nature of all things, the vision of love.
- Geburah (Might and Severity) is the creation of restorative conditions that are under the influence of the Archangel Khamael. On this Sephiroth all things are restored to their right way by whatever means are most expedient.
- Tiphereth (Beauty and Balance) Here we find mediating intelligence, the God–Goddess of knowledge. Ruled over by the Arch-

angel Mikal or Michael. Here is the know-how of life that keeps all the other powers in poise, and the vision of harmony and where the mystery of sacrifice is understood.

- Netzach (Victory and Achievement) The Sephiroth of the Divine principle in life that inspires all lives to achieve the highest possible station in life is watched over by the Archangel Elohim. Expressively, it is the human reflection of Divine love that satisfies all who search for such a reward.
- Hod (Glory and Honor) This is where we get our ideas of God from. The Archangel Raphael closely watches over this Sephiroth. Here we find the capacity for human healing and the splendor of honorable conduct.
- Malkuth (The Kingdom) Creation in our earthly sphere is carried out by Sandalaphon, from the Greek word meaning "co-brother," who is the other end of Metatron on Kether. Archangel Gabriel rules over this Sephiroth and maintains the movement of the universe. All that is matter and nature are collected within this sphere. Here the Kerubim encourage the qualities of patience, noble courage, lofty aspiration, and imagination—the keys to survival.

THE PILLARS

In addition to the Tree, on which the Sephiroth are placed, there are three pillars located on the Tree. The one to the left is the feminine pillar of severity, the middle neutral pillar is equilibrium, and the right pillar is masculine and the pillar of mercy.

As with everything related to the Qabalah, the esoteric ramifications of the pillars are vast. However, when looked at from a practical standpoint the pillars are mere reflections of our lives. We continually bounce from one to the other as we progress through life. There are times when we are too severe and go to the extreme with our thoughts or actions. This will usually pull us off course and toward the right and cause an immediate withdrawal of

The Pillar of
Form
Feminine
Severity
Restriction

The Pillar of
Balance

The Pillar of
Force
Masculine
Mercy
Expansion

our actions—often becoming too soft. This is usually when we try to regain our equilibrium and seek the middle path of balance.

The Qabalah teaches that by working with the Sephiroth, and their associated gods, angels, and energies we can learn to walk the middle path of balance and equilibrium. If we maintain a course upon this middle path we will achieve spiritual enlightenment and reunion with the Divine much faster and within fewer lifetimes. It is also suggested that by maintaining spiritual balance our daily lives will be richer and more fulfilling as well.

Most Wiccan groups that use the Qabalah tend to do so during meditation, in what is called path-working. This is a system of narrations or guided meditations that direct the consciousness along a specific path of knowledge. The idea is to gain wisdom from the journey and those gods and angels that you encounter while on the journey. The path-working always involves traveling to a specific astral place or temple, located between the Sephiroth. Each place and/or temple contains a rich and diverse set of spiritual symbolism that reflects on a past life or present day situation. The idea is to glean wisdom from these journeys that can then be applied to daily life or that can be used to enhance ritual work. In either case, each encounter opens the consciousness to higher forces and aids in spiritual progress.

13

Magick Rites and Spells

"It is our experience, as practicing Witches for twenty
years, that provided they are properly performed,
with an understanding of the principles involved—
yes, spells do work; if not always, then at least far
more often than either coincidence or alternative
explanations would allow."

—Janet and Stewart Farrar, *Spells and How They Work*

The following spells are ones which I have been teaching
people for years. They are simple to perform and don't require
impossible-to-find ingredients. In fact, most of the items used in
these spells are readily available in your own home or can be pur-
chased through any occult or New Age mail-order house. For those
spells that require special oils or incenses, the recipes are included
in Appendix II.

If you plan to do one of the spells presented here, read through
the spell several times. Be sure to make a ritual checklist and organize all that you need prior to the work. Most importantly, for the
spell to work and produce the desired results, you must do the
spell *exactly* as it has been scripted.

Last but not least, you are the best judge of what you need and are able to maintain. If you doubt what you are doing, or feel bad about it, then you have no business doing it. On the other hand, if it feels right and you are willing to accept responsibility for your actions then you have every right to move forward.

A Simple Love Spell

Items needed: love drawing oil, a pink candle, and a photograph of the one you desire.

Begin the spell by dressing the candle with the love drawing oil. As you dress the candle chant the following:

> *O goddess of love, hear my plea*
> *Bring everlasting love to me.*

Place the candle in its holder and light it. Place the photograph next to the lighted candle. Look at the photograph and focus your attention on it. Feel and think loving thoughts for this person whom you wish to attract. In your own words speak to the photograph as if the person were there. Tell them exactly how you feel and how you hope they feel the same. Take a few moments to reflect and think about what you want.

With all your attention focused on the photograph and the individual you wish to attract, chant the following nine times with great emotion:

> *Hail to thee goddess of love*
> *Shine down on me from above*
> *Bring now this love to me*
> *For this I will. So Mote It Be.*

A Spell to Attract Love

Items needed: one red seven-day knob candle, your birth stone, small piece of parchment paper, one tablespoon of basil, seven coriander seeds, one large spice jar decorated with red hearts.

Light the red seven-day knob candle. Hold the candle so that it will drip a pool of red wax onto the parchment paper. When you have a large enough pool shape the wax into a heart, inscribe the name of the one you desire into the soft wax and then press your birth stone into the center of the wax. As you do this, say the following:

> *Wax to heart now transformed*
> *Let this love now be warmed.*

Carefully fold the paper with the heart and birth stone on it. Place the paper, basil, and coriander seeds in the jar. Cap the jar and seal it with the candle wax. Allow the first knob of the candle to burn down, then extinguish the candle.

You will need to repeat this spell for six more nights. Each night light the candle (burning one knob each night) and place it next to the spice jar as you chant:

> *Fire, and passion, herb and stone*
> *I no longer shall be alone*
> *For your love shall come unto me*
> *For this I need. So Mote It Be.*

On the last day of the spell, as soon as the last knob has completely burned out, take the jar and bury it near the home of the one you desire. Turn and walk away and do not look back.

A CANDLE LOVE SPELL

Items needed: a piece of handwriting or photo of the one you desire, one red image candle, rose oil.

Begin by dressing the candle with the rose oil as you chant:

> *Bring unto me*
> *The love that I see*
> *That he (she) shall requite*
> *All my love from this night.*

Light the candle, and place it on top of the handwriting or picture. Allow the candle to burn for one hour and extinguish it. Each night for six consecutive nights repeat the spell, dressing the candle with the oil each time. On the last night of the spell allow the candle to burn out. Carry the handwriting or picture with you the next time you plan to see the one you desire.

A LOVE DRAWING TALISMAN

Items needed: customary magickal tools, salt and water, censor, one green silk pouch, the second pentacle of Venus (pictured) drawn on green paper, one green candle, Venus oil, Venus incense that is used to burn with coal.

Time this spell to begin on a Friday evening during the waxing of the moon. Prior to the spell inscribe the symbol for Venus (♀) on the silk pouch. Begin by casting the circle and consecrating the elements. Light the Venus incense and then dress the green candle with the Venus oil as you chant the following:

> *Candle flame and candle fire*
> > *Bring forth my desire*
> *Bring me love, bring me passion*
> > *As this talisman I now fashion.*

Pick up the talisman (the second pentacle or Venus) and hold it close to your heart. Visualize the person or type of person you wish to attract. Chant the following seven times:

> *By the powers of love and light*
> > *Release me from this lonely plight*
> *Grant to me passion and power*
> > *To bring forth love from this hour.*

Put the talisman in the bag and tie it shut. Sprinkle some incense on the coal, pass the talisman through the smoke of the incense, then over the flame of the candle, sprinkle with water, and then with salt. As you do this say:

> Air, Fire, Water, Earth
> To my desire now give birth.

Place the bag next to the candle. Take up the circle. Allow the candle to burn completely out. Carry the Venus talisman with you to attract love.

A Spell for Personal Success

Items needed: one gold candle, success oil, one small quartz crystal.

This spell may be done at any time, but for the best results begin it on a Sunday as close to high-noon as possible. Dress the gold candle with the success oil as you chant:

> Power of the rising sun
> Let success to me now come.

Place the candle and the crystal in a window, or some place where the sun will shine directly on it. Leave the candle until the sun has set. Place the candle and the crystal on your altar and light it as you say:

> Power of the morning light
> Of the candle and the flame.
> Take frustration from my sight
> Bring me now success and fame.

Allow the candle to burn for one hour. Repeat the spell for six consecutive days. On the last day allow the candle to completely burn out. Carry the crystal or place it in your desk at work.

A Jupiter Talisman for Prosperity

Items needed: fourth pentacle of Jupiter (pictured), Jupiter incense, clove oil, one orange candle, standard altar tools, four one dollar bills, a round box painted dark blue.

Begin by consecrating the elements and casting the circle. Pick up the blue candle and inscribe your name on it and the amount of money—be reasonable—that you would like have. Dress the candle with the clove oil as you chant:

> *Success and prosperity come to me*
> *This I will. So Mote It Be.*

Place the candle in its holder and light it. Gaze into the flame and visualize your desire.

Pick up the Jupiter pentacle, hold it in both hands and chant the following to energize it with your thoughts and feelings:

> *Honor, wealth, and prosperity*
> *Are what this talisman shall bring to me.*

Place the talisman under the blue candle. Take down the circle and leave the candle to burn for two hours. Repeat this spell four consecutive times. Each time dress the candle and repeat all of the above steps just as you did the first time. On the last day, place the talisman in the box along with the money. Whenever you need money, redo the spell.

First Pentacle of the Sun Prosperity Talisman

The First Pentacle of the Sun from the Key of Solomon transmits the countenance of the Almighty, at whose aspect all creatures obey, and the angelic spirits do reverence on bended knees. The face on the pentacle is that of the great angel Metatron.

Items needed: first pentacle of the Sun (pictured), a small gold pouch, marigold seeds.

On the first Sunday after the New Moon take your Pentacle and marigold seeds and go into the woods or garden. Stand so that you are in the direct rays of the sun. Hold up the pentacle and the seeds so that the rays of the sun shine directly on them. Charge them by chanting:

> *Almighty one of wealth and power*
> *Thou shalt be at my side from this hour*
> *Bring me wealth and blessings shower*
> *Let my prosperity from this time flower.*

Once the seeds have been charged, visualize your desire as you plant them. Place the pentacle in the gold pouch and carry it with you. Upon arising each morning, take out your pentacle and repeat the chant. Continue to do this until your seeds have grown into beautiful plants. You will then want to pick the flowers and dry them. Place one dried flower in your pouch with the pentacle. The others can be added to prosperity and money drawing oils and incenses.

A Simple Money Drawing Spell

This spell is especially useful if you are in the need of some quick cash. It can also be used to encourage a pay raise.

Items needed: one large green pillar candle, one piece of parchment paper.

Begin this spell by writing out the exact amount of money you need on the parchment paper. Set the candle on top of the paper and light it. Visualize the amount of money you need as you chant:

> *Money, money, come to me*
> *As I will. So Mote It Be.*

Allow the candle to burn for four hours. Repeat this spell until you have received the amount of money you asked for. This spell works best to get money from someone who owes it to you, a raise in pay, or for small amounts due you from forgotten sources.

THE PENTACLE PROTECTION SPELL

Items needed: pentacle pendant (pictured); protection oil; protection incense, charcoal, and censer; white candle; a bowl of salt; a bowl of water water; customary magickal tools.

Begin this spell on the night of the Full Moon. Consecrate the elements and cast your magick circle for protection. Place the pentacle in the bowl of salt. Dress the candle with the protection oil as you chant:

> *Candle of protection, power, and might*
> *Protect me from evil with your pure light.*

Light the candle. Sprinkle some protection incense on the charcoal. Take the pentacle from the salt and pass the pentacle through the elements as you say:

> *Let all of the elements now combine*
> *To protect my heart and my mind*
> *Let darkness and evil now fade away*
> *So that only good shall come my way.*

Place the pentacle next to the white candle. Take down the circle. Leave the candle to burn out completely. Immediately put the pentacle on, and wear it at all times. It is a good idea to recharge your pentacle at least once a month on the night of the Full Moon.

A SATURN PROTECTION SPELL

Items needed: one large black pillar candle; Saturn or protection oil; two mirror tiles; two Saturn pentacles (one pentacle should be large enough to cover the mirror, and the other small enough to carry in your purse or wallet); a picture of the person that is trying to harm you; customary altar tools; salt and water.

Begin by consecrating the elements and casting the magick circle. Place the picture of the person that is trying to harm you between the two mirrors—reflected sides facing in on each other. Take the large pentacle and place it on top of the mirror. Dress the black candle as you chant:

> *Candle black, and Saturn's power*
> *Reflect back evil from this hour*
> *All evil that is being sent to me*
> *Is now reflected by the law of three.*

Light the black candle and place it on top of the pentacle that is on the mirror. Pick up the small pentacle. Hold the pentacle in your strongest hand and chant:

> *For he(she) who causes me such pain*
> *Shall you suffer woe and shame.*

Now comes the tricky part. You must take down your circle, and leave the candle to burn completely out. I suggest placing it in a cauldron or large pot so that should it tip over it won't catch anything on fire. Next you must get the person that is causing you distress to step on or touch the pentacle in order to activate the spell. Once this person has come in contact with the pentacle, any negative actions or thoughts that are projected toward you will rebound on them three-fold.

A PEACEFUL HOME SPELL

Items needed: one blue candle, lavender oil, sandalwood incense.

This spell is very simple to do, and can be done at any time. It is especially useful if you will be entertaining people (such as in-laws) who do not necessarily always get along. Perform this spell one hour before your guests will arrive.

Begin by dressing the candle with the lavender oil. As you do, chant the following:

> *Queen of heaven, star of the sea*
> *Fill this house with love, and harmony.*
> *Blessed Goddess enthroned above*
> *Let all gather here in peace and love.*

Light the candle and place it in the room where everyone will be spending the majority of time. If you plan on serving dinner, use the candle as a part of your centerpiece; you can then move the candle to the room where you will be spending the rest of the evening. You will want to repeat the process using the incense. I suggest that you place the incense in the kitchen. Its subtle vibrations will then infuse the food and drink with love and harmony.

A SPELL FOR PEACE AND HARMONY

Items needed: one pink candle, one heart-shaped rose quartz, a small hand mirror.

Begin by lighting the pink candle. Place the candle on top of the mirror (reflected side up). Pick up the rose quartz and hold it close to your heart as you chant:

O blessed and reflected light
  Bring me peace from this night.
Let my mind and heart be free
  And filled with love and harmony.

Place the rose quartz on the mirror next to the pink candle. Take some time to reflect on what peace, love, and harmony feel like to you. Visualize an aura of pink, loving light surrounding you. Breathe in this pink light and let it fill your entire body, mind, soul with love. Sit with the candle for one hour. Extinguish the candle and carry the rose quartz with you. Repeat this spell whenever you feel the need for peace and harmony. This spell will charge your aura with love and make you a more attractive person.

The Invocations and the Rite of Union

The Invocation of the Goddess

This invocation is used at both Sabbat and Full Moon ceremonies, where it calls for the "Invocation to the Goddess." This is always done by a woman as the intention is to draw the essence of the Goddess down into the practitioner thereby intensifying the feminine energy within the circle. It is common practice if there is no woman available for one of the male participants to read the invocation rather than to actually do it. Please note that the God and Goddess names of Cernunnos and Cerridwen[1] have been used. These my be changed to suit the needs and pantheons of different traditions.

> *Thou who whispers gentle yet strong*
> *Thou for whom my soul doth long,*
> *By most men you are seldom seen*
> *Yet you ever reign, as virgin, mother, queen,*
> *Through the veil you pass with pride*
> *As I beckon thee now to be at my side,*
> > *Cerridwen!*

---

[1]Cerridwen is the Celtic mother goddess of grain. In our rituals we honor Cerridwen and Cernunnos. However, these names may be changed to match the pantheon being worked with. The intention is to draw down the god and goddess you are working with.

Thou who knows, thou who conceals
Thou who gives birth, thou who feels,
For you are the goddess, and mother to all
Pray thee now, come as I call,
Now through the mist, I hear your voice
And invoke thee most gracious goddess by choice,
    Cerridwen!

Thou who suffers as all men die
Doth with her victim in love lie,
For you are the goddess, and crone of despair
To our ending with you, we must share
I feel thy passion, and fell thy presence
I desire to be one with thy vital essence,
    Cerridwen!

I pray thee dancer of eternal bliss
Bestow upon me thy wondrous kiss
Let now thy light, love, and power
Descend, become one, with me this hour,
For you are the creatress of heaven and earth
To my soul and spirit you have given birth,
    Cerridwen!

The important factor is the transference of energy during the invocation. Therefore it is essential to work or call upon only those forces with which you are most familiar.

THE INVOCATION OF THE GOD

The invocation of the God, like that of the Goddess, is used during most Sabbat ceremonies or any ritual where the male god force is desired. It is of course performed by the male leading the group, or if there is none present, could be read aloud by one of the female members.

Father of death, father of night
Father of birth, father of light
Cernunnos, Cernunnos, Cernunnos
Come by Flame, Come by fire
Come now, whom we desire
Cernunnos, Cernunnos, Cernunnos

O' Horned one, O' ancient one
God of the sun, Bringer of light
The powers of Darkness put to flight.
O' Horned one, O' ancient one
Who comes from beyond the gates of death and birth
Come who gives life to all on earth

Come, I Invoke Thee
For you are Pan, Apollo, Cernunnos
Lord of Hades, Lord of death
You are them all, yet you are he.

Come, come my Lord, I beckon thee.
Come, come my lord, of wild delights
Come, join with us in these secret-mystic rites.
Come, come my lord, of fire and flame
As I call out your sacred, and holy name
Cernunnos, Cernunnos, Cernunnos

THE RITE OF UNION OR BLESSING
OF BREAD AND WINE

The Rite of Union, or blessing of bread and wine, is a common act in most Wiccan and some magickal traditions. It is during the Rite of Union that the wine and bread (or cake) are blessed, taking on the essence of the blood and body of the invoked deity or deities. In most Wiccan ceremonies, the wine is symbolic of the blood—the life essence of the Goddess, and the bread—the body or substance of the God. When the wine and bread are consumed by the participant, they are then transformed through the Divine symbolic attributes of the food.

For the Rite of Union you will need a chalice, athame, and two containers of wine—one red and one white (red and white grape juice may be used as a substitute).

The Rite of Union is performed by the male (LM) and female (LF) leaders of the group or Priest and Priestess. They will approach the altar, genuflect or bow. The (LM) will pick up the chalice and face the (LF), who will then pick up the two containers of wine, holding one in each hand. The (LM) kneels facing the (LF). The (LF) pours both the red and the white wine simultaneously into the chalice while saying:

> I pour the red and the white, that they shall mix, as life
> and death, joy and sorrow, peace and humility,
> and impart their essence of wonder unto all.

The (LM) remains kneeling, holding the wine-filled chalice and responds by saying:

> For I am the Father, lover, and Brother unto all.
> The bringer of life, the giver of death, before whom all
> time is ashamed.
> Let my spirit breathe upon you, and awaken the fires of
> inspiration deep within your soul.

The (LF) replaces the containers of wine on the altar. She will then pick up the athame. Slowly, she lowers the blade into the chalice while saying:

> For as this athame represents the male, and the God.

The (LM) responds by saying:

> And this chalice represents the female, and the Goddess.

The (LM) and (LF) respond in unison saying:

> *The two are conjoined to become one, in truth, power, and*
>   *wisdom.*
> *So Mote It Be.*

The (LM) now stands and takes a sip of the wine, he will then pass it to the (LF) saying:

> *Perfect love and perfect trust.*

The (LF) takes a sip, repeats "Perfect love and perfect trust," and then passes the wine back to the (LM) who will then pass it to each member in the group. Each member of the group responds by saying "Perfect love and perfect trust."

THE SOLITARY RITE OF UNION

This is a simplified version of the actual Rite of Union and is used by those who practice as solitary Witches. The practitioner will fill the chalice with red and white wine before the ritual. When the time comes to perform the Rite of Union he or she will face the altar, genuflect or bow, and pick up the chalice. While holding the chalice in offering he or she will say:

> *My Lord is the power and force of all life,*
> *My Lady is the vessel through which all life flows.*
> *My Lord is life and death,*
> *My Lady is birth and renewal.*
> *The Sun brings forth life,*
> *The Moon holds it in darkness.*

He or she will now plunge the athame into the chalice saying:

> *For as the Lance is to the male,*
> *So the Grail is to the female,*
> *And together they are conjoined to become one*
> *In Truth, power, and wisdom.*

He or she will now drink the wine in honor of the God and Goddess.

Blessing the Cakes (Bread)

Blessing the bread or ritual cakes takes on the same significance as does the blessing of the wine. During the blessing, the vital essence of the God is drawn down into the bread or cake so that all present may partake of the deity's essence.

The act of blessing the bread will be done by the (LF) and the (LM). The (LF) will pick up the plate of bread and face the (LM) who will then place his hands over the plate. The (LF) speaks first saying:

> *Behold the sovereignty of our Divine King*
> *Beloved son and lover*
> *Radiant and everlasting light*
> *Guardian of the souls of man who rises triumphant from*
> *   the tomb.*

The (LM) will respond by saying:

> *We give honor to thee O sacrificed God*
> *Who through the Mother, grants eternity.*
> *By shedding your blood upon the land,*
> *All are transformed through your passion*
> *As they pass through the gates of judgement.*

The (LM) will pick up a piece of bread and hold it over the plate, in unison the (LM) and (LF) say:

> *Let now the mystery be revealed*
> *Of the light of the Lord within,*
> *Who in the shadow of the Goddess*
> *Will ever reign supreme.*
> *So Mote It Be!*

The (LM) take a piece of bread saying: "Perfect love and perfect trust," the (LF) then takes a piece of bread and responds by saying: "Perfect love and perfect trust." The bread is then passed among the members of the group, just as the wine was, and each member responds by saying: "Perfect love and perfect trust."

SOLITARY BREAD BLESSING

Before ritual the practitioner will place the bread or cake on a small plate or on top of the pentacle. As soon as the wine has been blessed the practitioner will bless the bread by holding his or her hands over the bread and saying:

O Great Lord of Heavenly power
Whose presence reigns from above
Be with me in this ritual hour
And grace this bread with your love.
So Mote It Be!

As with all Wiccan rituals and celebrations, the blessing of bread and wine is not written in granite. If you have blessings that you like better than the ones presented here, by all means use them. You may also amend the rites written here to fit in with your traditional practices. The important thing is to feel comfortable with what you are doing, and to memorize as much of the repetitious activities as possible. For the most part, the casting of the circle, summoning and dismissing Guardians, the Rite of Union, and Blessing of the Bread should all be committed to memory prior to working with a group or celebrating Sabbats.

Appendix II

Correspondences, Charts, and Recipes

ELEMENTAL CORRESPONDENCES

AIR

Direction:	East
Archangel:	Raphael
Qualities:	Light, intellect, new beginnings
Color:	Blue
Meaning:	To know
Zodiac:	Gemini, Aquarius, Libra
Tattvic symbol:	Circle
Season:	Spring
Magickal tool:	Wand or dagger
Animal:	Eagle
Symbols:	Sky, wind, clouds, incense
Elemental spirit:	Sylphs
Elemental king:	Paralda
Positive characteristics:	Intelligence, mind, psychic abilities
Negative characteristics:	Lack of communication, gossip, memory problems

FIRE

Direction:	South
Archangel:	Michael
Qualities:	Activity, force, willpower
Color:	Red
Meaning:	To will
Zodiac:	Aries, Leo, Sagittarius
Tattvic symbol:	Triangle
Season:	Summer
Magickal tool:	Dagger or wand
Animal:	Lion
Symbols:	Fire, sun, passion, candles
Elemental spirit:	Salamanders
Elemental king:	Djyn
Positive characteristics:	Energy, enthusiasm, will, strength
Negative characteristics:	Greed, vengeance, ego, jealousy

WATER

Direction:	West
Archangel:	Gabriel
Qualities:	Heavy, passive, receptivity
Color:	Green
Meaning:	To dare
Zodiac:	Cancer, Scorpio, Pisces
Tattvic symbol:	Crescent Moon
Season:	Fall
Magickal tool:	Chalice
Animal:	Snake, Scorpion
Symbols:	Waves, bodies of water, cups
Elemental spirit:	Undines
Elemental king:	Niksa
Positive characteristics:	Sensitivity, compassion, grace
Negative characteristics:	Overly emotional, insecurities, lack of self-esteem

EARTH

Direction:	North
Archangel:	Auriel (Uriel)
Qualities:	Stability, growth, manifestation
Color:	Yellow
Meaning:	To keep silent
Zodiac:	Taurus, Virgo, Capricorn
Tattvic symbol:	Square
Season:	Winter
Magickal tool:	Pentacle
Animal:	Bull
Symbols:	Mountains, forest, stone, salt
Elemental spirit:	Gnomes and trolls
Elemental king:	Gob
Positive characteristics:	Endurance, reliability, material world
Negative characteristics:	Materialistic, non-progressive and lazy

HERBS OF THE ZODIAC

Aries (The Ram): Fire, Cardinal: Allspice, cactus, dragons blood, pepper

Taurus (The Bull): Earth, Fixed: Alfalfa, honeysuckle, primrose, tulip

Gemini (The Twins): Air, Mutable: Almond, clover, lavender, pine

Cancer (The Crab): Water, Cardinal: Lemon balm, cucumber, lilac, thyme

Leo (The Lion): Fire, Fixed: Basil, coriander, hyssop, tobacco

Virgo (The Virgin): Earth, Mutable: Corn, magnolia, vetivert, wheat

Libra (The Scales): Air, Cardinal: Broom, eyebright, lily of the valley, mint

Scorpio (The Scorpion): Water, Fixed: Belladonna, hemlock, lotus, willow

Sagittarius (The Archer): Fire, Mutable: Asafoetida, garlic, rosemary, wormwood

Capricorn (The Goat): Earth, Cardinal: Cypress, patchouly, mugwort, vervain

Aquarius (The Water Bearer): Air, Fixed: Benzoin, linden, mistletoe, papyrus

Pisces (The Fishes): Water, Mutable: Crocus, heather, myrrh, yarrow

CORRESPONDENCES FOR THE DAYS OF THE WEEK

Sunday, corresponds to the **sun**, and the first day of the week. It represents high masculine energy and is a very good time for individual, positive, creative works. Sunday is a good time to begin spells that are aimed at acquiring money, health, friendship, and patronage for business.

Monday, the second day of the week aligns with the **moon**. This is a day of high feminine energy, a good time to develop self-expression, seek inspiration, and work to enhance psychic abilities. Monday is a good time to begin spells that deal with initiating changes and personal growth of the feminine aspect.

Tuesday, belongs to **Mars**, the god of war. This is a time of dynamic energy and pure raw power. Tuesday is a good time to begin spells that will overcome rivalry or malice; develop physical strength and courage, or will help protect one's property and investments. It is also a good time for military matters and anything that requires a lot of force, power, and energy to activate.

Wednesday, is associated with **Mercury** and the ability to communicate. The power of Mercury is what helps you get your ideas out there. Wednesday is a good time to do spells where communication is involved since Mercury is used to influence others, and help them see things your way. Spells that deal with work and career are best done on Wednesday.

Thursday, corresponds to the planet **Jupiter**. It deals with expansion, idealism, and ambition. Jupiter will help you attain friendships. Thursday is a good time to do spells for career success and situations concerned with money. Legal transactions are best dealt with during Jupiter.

Friday, belongs to **Venus**—the goddess of love. All things concerned with love, attraction, friendships, and lust come under the jurisdiction of Venus. Friday is the best time to work spells that involve sensual and sexual attraction or friendships

Saturday, the last day of the week is associated with **Saturn**, and the first law of karma (limitation). Magically, Saturn is the tester, and the principle of learning through trial and error. Saturn spells should be used to preserve, stabilize, and crystallize ability—the ability to discipline the self.

CORRESPONDENCES FOR THE MONTHS OF THE YEAR

Month	Attribute	Color	Stone
January	Protection	Black	Onyx
February	Motivation	Turquoise	Aquamarine
March	Victory	Purple	Amethyst
April	Opportunity	Red	Garnet
May	Progress	Blue	Lapis Lazuli
June	Devotion	Green	Aventurine
July	Control	Yellow	Diamond
August	Unity	Brown	Agate
September	Harvest	Gold	Topaz
October	Transformation	Clear	Diamond
November	Psychic	Dark Blue	Sapphire
December	Insight	White	Chalcedony

INCENSE AND OIL

To make the following incenses you will need to combine the listed ingredients in small bags or jars and label and store them appropriately. For the oils, purchase small glass or plastic vials from health food or New Age shops, along with an eye-dropper and labels. These incenses will be in a powder form so you should also get charcoal tablets for when you use them.

Love Drawing Incense

A small piece of rose quartz
One small rose bud
¼ cup red base
1 tsp. basil
2 tbsps. rose buds
½ tsp. rose oil

Love Drawing Oil

1 part rose oil
1 part musk oil
1 drop cherry oil
A small piece of rose quartz
One small rose bud

High Altar Oil

1 part frankincense oil
1 part myrrh oil
1 part sandalwood oil

High Altar Incense

¼ cup brown base
¼ cup frankincense
¼ cup sandalwood
¼ cup myrrh
1 tsp. frankincense oil
1 tsp. myrrh oil

1 clear quartz crystal in the container

Protection Incense

¼ cup black base
¼ cup patchouly leaves
2 tbsps. Dragons Blood resin
2 tbsps. Copal
2 tbsps. patchouly oil
2 tbsps. frankincense oil
2 drops camphor oil

Place a piece of black onyx in the box with the ingredients

Protection Oil

1 part patchouly oil
2 parts frankincense oil
1 part camphor oil
2 parts sandalwood oil
1 part rosemary oil

Success Incense

¼ cup gold base
2 tbsps. marigolds
2 tbsps. myrrh
1 tsp. ambergris oil
½ tsp. myrrh oil

Success Oil

1 part ambergris oil
1 part myrrh oil
1 part storax oil
1 pinch marigolds
1 pinch gold glitter

Protection Oil

1 part patchouly oil
2 parts frankincense oil
1 part camphor oil
2 parts sandalwood oil
1 part rosemary oil

BIBLIOGRAPHY

Beyerl, Paul. *Master Book of Herbalism*. Custer, Wa.: Phoenix Publishing Co., 1984.

Bias, Clifford. *Ritual Book of Magic*. York Beach, Me.: Samuel Weiser, 1982.

Dunwich, Gerina. *Exploring SpellCraft*. Franklin Lakes, N.J.: New Page Books, 2001.

Goodwin, Joscelyn. *Mystery Religions in the Ancient World*. San Francisco, Ca.: Harper & Row, 1981.

Green, Marion. *A Witch Alone*. Wellingborough, England: The Aquarian Press, 1991.

Green, Marion. *The Elements of Natural Magic*. London: Elements Books, 1992.

Heisler, Roger. *Path to Power, It's All in Your Mind*. York Beach, Me.: Samuel Weiser, 1990.

Huson, Paul. *Mastering Witchcraft*. New York: G.P. Putnam and Sons, 1970.

Liddell, S. and MacGregor Mathers. *The Key of Solomon the King*. York Beach, ME, Samuel Weiser, 1974.

Sabrina, Lady. *The Witches Master Grimoire*. Franklin Lakes, N.J.: New Page Books, 2000.

Sabrina, Lady. *Exploring Wicca*. Franklin Lakes, N.J.: New Page Books, 2000.

Sabrina, Lady. *Reclaiming the Power, the How and Why of Practical Ritual Magic*. St. Paul, Minn.: Llewellyn Publications, 1992.

Skelton, Robin. *The Practice of Witchcraft Today*. Secaucus, N.J.: Citadel Press, 1990.

Skelton, Robin. *Spell Craft*. York Beach, Me.: Samuel Weiser, 1978.

Skelton, Robin. *Talismanic Magic*. York Beach, Me.: Samuel Weiser, 1985.

Telesco, Patricia. *Seasons of the Sun*. York Beach, Me.: Samuel Weiser, 1996.

Telesco, Patricia. *A Charmed Life*. Franklin Lakes, N.J.: New Page Books, 2000.

Valiente, Doreen. *Witchcraft for Tomorrow*. New York: St. Martins Press, 1978.

INDEX

179